在线语料库实用教程

张 蕊 编著

图书在版编目(CIP)数据

在线语料库实用教程 / 张蕊编著. — 西安：西安交通大学出版社,2022.10(2024.8重印)
ISBN 978-7-5693-2848-6

Ⅰ.①在… Ⅱ.①张… Ⅲ.①语料库-语言学-教材 Ⅳ.①H0

中国版本图书馆 CIP 数据核字(2022)第 198183 号

书　　名	在线语料库实用教程 Zaixian Yuliaoku Shiyong Jiaocheng
编　　著	张　蕊
策划编辑	杨　璠
责任编辑	杨　璠
责任校对	张静静
出版发行	西安交通大学出版社 (西安市兴庆南路1号　邮政编码710048)
网　　址	http://www.xjtupress.com
电　　话	(029)82668357　82667874(市场营销中心) (029)82668315(总编办)
传　　真	(029)82668280
印　　刷	西安五星印刷有限公司
开　　本	787 mm×1092 mm　1/16　印张 9　字数 210千字
版次印次	2022年10月第1版　2024年8月第2次印刷
书　　号	ISBN 978-7-5693-2848-6
定　　价	48.00元

如发现印装质量问题,请与本社市场营销中心联系。
订购热线:(029)82665248　(029)82665249
投稿热线:(029)82668804
读者信箱:phoe@qq.com

版权所有　侵权必究

目 录

第一章 语料库使用简介 …………………………………………………… (1)

第二章 频率 ………………………………………………………………… (26)

第三章 关键词索引 ………………………………………………………… (44)

第四章 词语搭配 …………………………………………………………… (55)

第五章 类联接 ……………………………………………………………… (70)

第六章 关键词索引分布 …………………………………………………… (82)

第七章 主题词分析 ………………………………………………………… (84)

第八章 语料库语言学的应用:词典编纂 ………………………………… (92)

第九章 数据驱动语法 ……………………………………………………… (99)

第十章 话语标记语 听者身份 关系语言 ……………………………… (105)

第十一章 语言变体 ………………………………………………………… (117)

第十二章 语料库和语言教学 ……………………………………………… (126)

第十三章 语料库设计 ……………………………………………………… (136)

参考文献 ……………………………………………………………………… (140)

第一章 语料库使用简介

📝 语料工具

- ●杨百翰大学语料库(BYU)
- ●英国国家语料库(British National Corpus，BNC)
- ●当代美国英语语料库(COCA)
- ●《时代》周刊语料库(TIME)

👤 教学内容

欢迎参加"语料库语言学"初级课程的学习。在这门课中，我们将带领大家了解语料库语言学的一些基本概念，熟悉一些可用的在线语料库资源。

这门课主要讲什么？首先，我们要了解一下什么是语料库，特别是一些差异巨大的在线语料库。其次，我们会了解语料库语言学特有的搜索工具，比如关键词索引检索、词语搭配以及关键词检索，我们也会探索如何使用各种语料库来研究诸如英语中的词汇、语法、话语和语言变体等问题。

什么是语料库？corpus 在拉丁语中原来是"身体"的意思，语料库就是语言的身体，语言的任何一部分。但是现在，语料库被认为是很多的自然语言，用电子的方式，也就是机器可读的形式，储存在电脑中。正因为它的存储方式是电子的，我们才可以设计工具来快速、轻松地进行检索。语料库就是储存在电脑中的大量书面或者口头形式的自然语言，可以使用不同种类的软件来检索。

谁会对语料库感兴趣呢？早期的语料库语言学家，也就是词典编纂者，使用语料库来收集词典编纂的依据。传统的词典编纂者收集并编辑词典编写需要的数据。读者阅读大量的书面材料，将摘抄的小纸条送给编辑们，然后由编辑筛选，寻找未收录的单词，或者已收录单词的最新意义。这个过程可能要花费几十年，甚至几代人的时间。语料库带来了革命性的变化，现在使用计算机语料库，我们可以快速地搜索新词和旧词的新义。我们可以关注到单词意义中一些被忽略的方面。

现在开始第一个活动。首先，请想一想形容词 seedy 是什么意思，写下你对该词的定义，以及经常和 seedy 一起使用的名词。

如果你在权威词典中查 seedy 这个词，比如在牛津英语辞典的网站www.oed.com 上查

这个单词,会找到五个意项,最主要的两个是:

① a. Abounding in seed, full of seed.(多种子的)
   b. Used to designate the male hop-plant.(用来指代蛇麻草的雄株)

② a. Shabby, ill-looking.(破旧的,衣衫褴褛的)
   b. Unwell, poorly, "not up to the mark", spec. as a result of excessive eating or drinking(指无精打采的,尤其是过度饮食导致的状态)

还有其他的三个更专业的意项:③吹玻璃;④品尝白兰地酒;⑤羊毛。

现在我们在拥有 1 亿词汇的英国国家语料库(British National Corpus)中了解 seedy 这个单词。

在线练习 1

我们来进行第一个活动。

1. 访问网址:http://corpus.byu.edu/bnc,如图 1.1 所示。

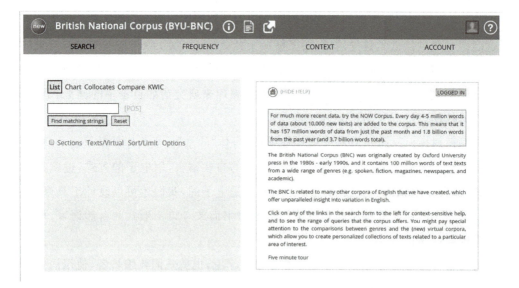

图 1.1

2.在菜单栏,点击 List,如图 1.2 所示。

图 1.2

3.在检索处输入 seedy,然后点击"Find matching strings"(找到匹配字母串)或按回车键。

4.你会看到在包含 1 亿词条的英国国家语料库中 seedy 这个词的出现频率。这个频率是 115,如图 1.3 所示。

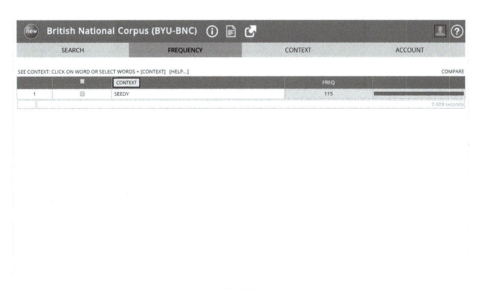

图 1.3

5.点击检索结果中的 seedy 这个词,看看它在语境中是怎么使用的,如图 1.4 所示。用笔记下 seedy 修饰的名词,如 affair、hotel、bars 等,再想一下这些名词有没有什么共同之处。

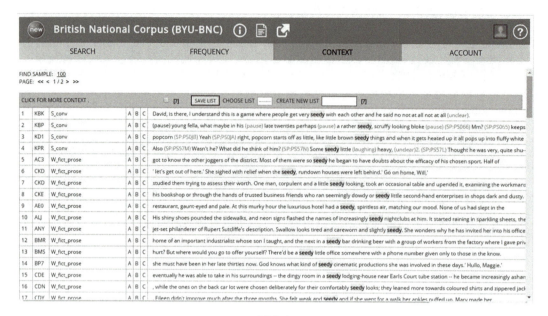

图 1.4

然后我们再在当代美国英语语料库中对 seedy 这个词进行检索,看看两个语料库中检索出的结果有何不同。当代美国英语语料库(COCA)的容量为 5 亿 2000 万个单词。访问网址 http://corpus.byu.edu/coca/后重复上述步骤 2 到 5 得到检索结果,如图 1.5 所示,观察在美式英语和英式英语中有哪些词是都可以用 seedy 来修饰的。

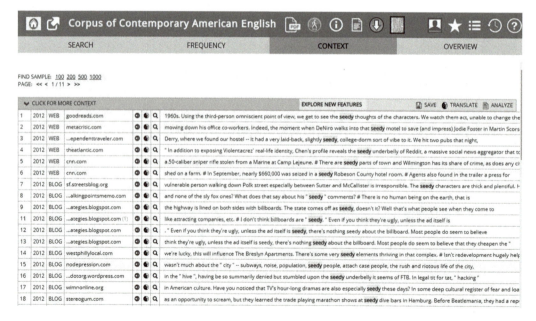

图 1.5

以上检索的结果与你预料的一致还是让你大吃一惊？seedy 这个词最初与植物结籽相关，但如果语境中没有植物的概念时，seedy 表达的意思就是衣衫褴褛或不注意修饰。英国国家语料库的检索结果与词典中的这个定义一致。比如在这个句子中："Harold Macmillan's seedy and stagnant Britain."这里的 seedy 意为破旧，乌烟瘴气的。

在英国国家语料库中你会发现 seedy 的用法很多时候与性有关，比方说：

> seedy affair
>
> seedyporn photos
>
> seedy abortionist
>
> a rake's progress of late nights, seedy bars and relentless beer bellies
>
> the seedy world of prostitution
>
> the film-maker's seedy little wife, pornpously and unseductively nude
>
> seedy northern beauty contest
>
> a seedy image of people who useporn
>
> gave up her seedy career and wrote an expose of theporn business

当然，在 BNC 语料库中也能找到 seedy 与性无关的一些用法，比如说用于描述英国演员 William Hay 所饰演的教师角色，a seedy, blustering and ineffectual teacher，这里的 seedy 意为衣衫褴褛的；还有 seedy grass-heads caught in my socks 中的 seedy 意为植物的籽。但是与性相关的例子占了绝大多数。这些例子充分表明在当代英语中，seedy 一词含有性方面不受欢迎的含义，这一点通过语境表现得非常明显，无须明示。比如说 business friends who ran seemingly dowdy or seedy little second-hand enterprises in shops dark and dusty.

值得注意的是，在线词典 Oxford English Dictionary 对该词的解释最接近的恐怕就是 shabby(寒碜的)或者 ill as a result of excessive drink(因饮酒过度的原因而不健康的)。

另外一个在线词典 Macmillan Dictionary(http://www.macmillandictionary.com)受到语料库的影响就比较大。Macmillan 词典给出的主要意义是：connected with activities that are illegal or morally wrong, and often looking dirty or unpleasant（与违法行为或不道德行为相关的，看上去肮脏且令人不愉快的），如图 1.6 所示。

然后，我们再来看看语料库数据是不是和我们的直觉以及不同词典中的定义相吻合。当然，我们对词语的直觉也是因为我们经常看到或听到这些单词，比如说我们阅读或听一百万个单词的时候就能碰到一个 seedy。这样我们的大脑中就将这个单词和大量的语境联系起来，但是我们无法清楚地回忆出这些单词的语境信息。约翰·辛克莱（John Sinclair）

(1991)[100]是现代语料库语言学的先驱,他说道:"当你同时观察很多语言现象的时候,语言与平时的感觉就不同了。"

图 1.6

以上介绍的只是通过语料库探索语言的一种可能,随着课程的深入,我们还会学习到更多的语料库语言学的实际应用。但在那之前,我们先来思考关于语料库设计的一些基本问题。我们之前介绍过,语料库就是一系列储存在电脑中的自然语言,但是,是不是什么自然语言都可以成为语料库的一部分呢?如果我们从网络上下载了一些文本,那会是语料库吗?多少语言文本才可以成为一个语料库?是不是所有的语料库都是一样的?

无论是否是在线语料库,我们在使用语料库之前都需要注意它的设计,因为任何一个可靠的语料库都不仅仅是随机地将语言材料扔到一起。自从20世纪60年代出现第一个电脑语料库以来,各种各样的语料库被开发出来。接下来我们来了解一些主要的语料库类型。

首先,是通用语料库和专门语料库,像英国国家语料库和当代美语语料库就属于通用语料库。通用语料库尝试尽可能完整地呈现一种语言,不管是口语形式还是书面语形式。专门语料库,顾名思义,它并不试图反映某一个语言变体的全貌。像书面新闻、肥皂剧中使用的语言、国会演说或者大学中的口头话语类型等都属于语言变体。专门语料库包括书面新闻的《时代》周刊语料库(TIME),电视剧本的《肥皂剧》语料库(SOAP),英国议会演讲的《英国议会议事录》语料库(Hansard)以及密歇根大学录制的口语语料库(MICASE)等。

其次,代表性问题非常重要,但也非常棘手。只有当语料库包括了某种语言或语言的变体时,我们才能对这种语言的通用情况或特殊语言变体做出正确的概括。没有人可以根据苏格兰英语语料库来总结出新加坡英语的使用特征,我们也不能根据书面语语料库来总结出口语的词汇使用特点,反之亦然。同样,我们不能因为科学文本语料库中经常出现某种语法结构就推论说这种结构在更大范围的语言使用中也是频繁出现的。

我们构建有代表性的语料库是为了降低由于语言数据库不全或者有偏差而做出错误的结论。语料库语言学强调语料库要有代表性，但是学者一直没有就语料库能否实现完美的代表性这个问题取得一致看法，也就更无法探讨理想语料库的组成成分了。语料库中的书面语和口语的黄金比例是多少？在或长或短的时间内，像《圣经》、英国女王演讲或者美国总统演讲、罗琳(J. K. Rowling)的小说、阿加莎·克里斯蒂(Agatha Christie)或苏珊·柯林斯(Suzanne Collins)的小说、头版新闻文章等类型的文本，它们的读者或听者范围很广，人数众多；但其他一些文本的读者或听者人数较少，或群体较小，比如说专业的学术著作、赛马会的报告、乡村小教堂中进行的布道活动等。那么，我们如何才能保证不同年纪、性别、职业、种族、宗教、成长环境的人群的声音在语料库中得到体现呢？

简单地说，有代表性的语料库就是语料库中收录了各种语域和体裁的大量文本。大多数通用语料库至少会尝试反映不同类型口语和书面语的特点，其中的文本涵盖全部，从轻松随意的谈话到斟词酌句的法律文本。看看当代英语语料库，你会看到其中包括了不同语域的语言，如口语、小说、杂志、报纸以及学术英语。这个语料库貌似已经相当全面了，但是我们看看还有没有什么不足。COCA 中的语料都属于"公共话语(public discourse)"，即使是 COCA 中的口语部分也是转录自媒体节目中的真实话语。但是还有一些本质上非常私人的语言怎么办呢？比如说私人日记、亲密对话、你在组装自己的书架时一边阅读说明书一边自言自语时说的话，这些话语不纳入通用语料库，是否合理？BNC 中涵盖的口语题材特点就比 COCA 要更多样化一点。但是，获取并公开"私人话语"显然有很多困难。语料库的设计者必须利用手头的资料，并尽可能使其具有代表性。

在通用语料库之外，还有专门语料库，比如说《时代》周刊语料库，其中的所有语料都取自《时代》周刊中的文章。语料库的设计者是马克·戴维斯(Mark Davies)，他按十年为一组整理了从 20 世纪 20 年代到 90 年代的所有语料。这个语料库全部来自书面报道。由于其时间跨度长达 90 多年，《时代》周刊语料库也具备历时语料库的功能，它向我们呈现语言是如何不断变化的。接下来我们来完成一个小活动，探索下美式英语的变化。

在线练习 2

我们一起来看看《时代》周刊(Time)的语言变化。这是一个历时的美国记者报道语料库，很好地展示了那个时期的语言变化，可以被用来研究语言学和文化方面的问题，比如：外来词素 nik 是什么时候被引入美国英语当中的？在记者报道文本中 nik 的一系列用法是什么？在英语中都有哪些意思？

1. 访问 http://corpus.byu.edu/time。
2. 键入检索项 *nik（如果你想检索它的复数形式，可以键入 *nik *），如图 1.7 所示。

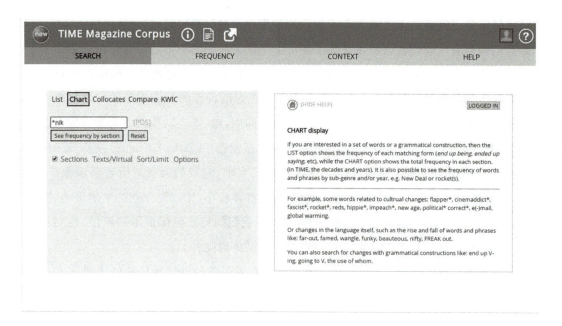

图 1.7

3. 在菜单栏里点击 Chart(图表)。

4. 结果会告诉你从 20 世纪 20 年代到 21 世纪初所有带-nik 后缀的词出现的频率，如图 1.8所示。是不是跟你预测的一样？这个后缀出现的频率是一直在保持还是有所下降？点击列表里的任意年份，在图标下方你会看到每一个年份的检索结果。其中有一些干扰项，应把它们剔除，比如人名中含有-nik 的。有没有词汇包含-nik 作为小后缀？用这种方法再检索其他几个后缀，如 * ista，像 Fashionista。

SECTION (CLICK FOR SUB-SECTIONS) (SEE ALL SECTIONS AT ONCE)	FREQ	SIZE (M)	PER MIL	CLICK FOR CONTEXT (SEE ALL)
1920s	36	7.6	4.72	
1930s	60	12.7	4.74	
1940s	123	15.5	7.96	
1950s	478	16.8	28.47	
1960s	297	16.1	18.47	
1970s	117	13.6	8.61	
1980s	164	11.4	14.42	
1990s	158	9.7	16.23	
2000s	77	6.4	11.98	
TOTAL	1,510			SEE ALL TOKENS

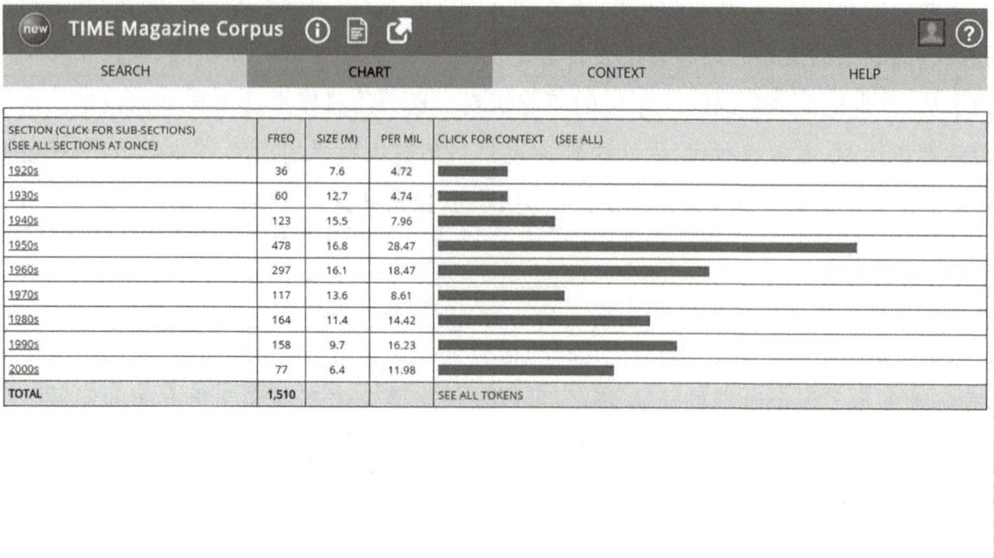

图 1.8

我们一起再检索一遍。在《时代》周刊语料库中键入检索项 * nik，你会找到所有以-nik结尾的单数名词。点击 Chart，看看每一部分的频率，你会发现前半个世纪中，-nik 出现的频率相对较少，在 20 世纪 50 年代急剧增长，然后逐年缓慢下降。

如果我们以每一个十年里的前 100 个词为例，词义的变化会更加明显。

在 20 世纪 20 年代到 20 世纪 40 年代期间，我们主要看到从俄语中直接借用的带有-nik 这个后缀的词用来指人，如 udarnik（突击手）、voyentechnik（技术员），你可能意识到了-nik 来自俄语，后缀意为"小"，还被用于绰号指具有某种特性的人。

到 20 世纪 50 年代，"小"这个意思继续被用于构成专有名词和绰号，例如，loverboynik 指演艺明星李伯拉斯（Liberace），他被认为是美男子的代表。这个后缀还意为"微小的""渺小的"。1957 年发生了一件全球性的具有深远意义的事，那就是苏联发射了第一颗人造卫星。这颗卫星的名字叫"Little Moon"（小月亮），俄语是 Sputnik。随后，这个词很快在杂志中频频出现。

到 20 世纪 60 年代，Sputnik 还很热门，同时此时又出现了带有-nik 这个词缀的新词：beatnik、pre-beatnik、sicknik、sugar-beatnik、goatnik、court-nik、bleatnik。

到 20 世纪 60 年代，美国社会变革时代到来，-nik 这个后缀开始跟"另类生活方式和另类价值观以及狂热"相关联。

到 20 世纪 70 年代，-nik 这个后缀的使用开始衰落，而 beatnik 这个词幸存下来，此外又出现了几个新词如 kibbutznik、refusenik。

20 世纪 80 年代至 21 世纪初，-nik 这个后缀主要用于人名，同时出现了一些新词，如 no-goodnik、peacenik、Greenpeacenik。

《时代》周刊语料库可以展示给我们一些语料库时代之前无法探寻的东西，即因社会变化而变化的语言，就像太空竞赛中发射卫星这个事件所带来的影响。《时代》周刊语料库表明俄语后缀在 20 世纪 50 年代早期就出现在美国英语里被用于表达讽刺、挖苦的含义，然而直到 20 世纪 50 年代后期出现 Sputnik 这个词时，才使得"渺小"这个含义变得普遍起来。20 世纪 60 年代是社会动荡、价值观改变的时代，这一时期出现了很多新词，通常形容某人的波希米亚风格或者危险分子。20 世纪 70 年代往后是一些主要新词的存活期，如 beatnik，同时又出现了一些新词，但是这个后缀产生新词的影响力逐渐消退。

尽管这是一个非常具体的例子，但却告诉我们跟英语有关的很多东西。正如分析所表明的，英语的趋势是吸收一定的外来语的语法标记，然后用它们来表明看法、意见。

到目前为止，我们已经了解了通用语料库和专门的语料库了。《时代》周刊专业语料库还是一个历时的语料库，它随着时间的推移，抽取样本语言，所以在专业期刊领域里我们可以看到语言变化是如何起作用的。另一个更加综合性的历时语料库是美国英语历史语料库（COHA），这个语料库主要关注从 1810 年到 20 世纪初的美国英语。它的语域涉及小说、杂志、报纸和其他非小说体裁。很明显，历时语料库很少涉及口语语料，COHA 关注"公共话语"，尽管其范围有局限性，但对于广泛的语言来说它比《时代》周刊更具代表性，并且比英语国家语料库(1980s—1990s)更具历时性。英语国家语料库被认为是共时语料库,因为在这个语料库里语言被限制在一个较短的时间范围内。

最原始的英语国家语料库被认为是静态语料库,目前尚未更新,会在以后进行更新,而美国当代英语语料库会定时更新,每年会定期增加2000万个单词。美国当代英语语料库在扩大,但是语料库的设计保持不变,所以可以认为它是一个小语料库,在这个动态语料库里可以探寻语言的最新变化。如果想获得最新的语言变化,可以使用另一个动态语料库,网络新闻语料库(News on the Web),这个语料库目前包括3亿词汇数据,它的语域仅限于网上期刊。这个语料库的特点是每天增加400万到500万个单词。

你可能会问一个问题:一个语料库应该有多大?语料库的大小是一个单独的但又跟语料库的代表性密切相关的问题。如果你想编一本词典,那所需的语料库要很大,通常要容纳10亿个词。O'Keeffe等(2007)[4]认为要获取足够的跟bargain搭配的介词,需要在语料库搜索一千万个词。"对于是什么构成了大的或小的语料库,取决于这个语料库是口语语料库还是书面语语料库以及它想代表什么。对于口语语料库来说,任何超过1000万个词的语料库都被认为是大的。对于书面语语料库来说,任何少于500万词的语料库都是小的。"

很多频繁出现的词汇或核心词汇、语言的构成和特点都可以用语料库来分析,即使是只有几万词的语料库。规模跟设计一样,是语料库的一个特点,要符合语料库的创建目的。对于为了语言学习而建的语料库,Chambers(2007)[9]说:"有一点很清楚,尽管语料库语言学家希望语料库越大越好,这样可以支持研究者探寻难以捉摸的代表性,但是他们中那些关注课堂应用的研究者以及和学习者一起工作过的研究者已经意识到小语料库的作用。"

小语料库也很有用,如果你观察一个特定语言变体的频率特点(一些常见的语法特点),如商务报告,在这种情况下,语料库没有必要很大。即使是这样,有些语料库真的非常大,例如网络新闻语料库和全球网络英语语料库(GLoWbE),含有1.9亿个词汇。当然,初学者最好能接触到大的语料库,因为人们普遍认为语料库越大越可靠,尤其是对于那些不常见的语言特点,全面的理解很重要。不仅是规模,还有所使用的语料库的设计,以及在哪个语料库中能发现这些特点。当然,选择哪个语料库,很大程度上还是取决于你想让语料库回答什么问题。

你想问的问题跟你决定用什么样的语料库密切相关。你是想了解美国英语和英国英语有什么不同,还是苏格兰英语、加拿大英语、澳大利亚英语、新加坡英语或其他英语变体?这个语料库是不是具有代表性?包不包括公共话语和个人话语、书面语和口语?每个语域在语料库中的比重是多少?你对书面语感兴趣还是对口语感兴趣?如果使用专业语料库,在所研究的方面是不是具有代表性?在语料库设计中你使用的数据收集和整理原则是什么?你是对某个特定时期的语言感兴趣(能否使用静态语料库)还是对现在正在使用的语言感兴趣?你真的像词典编纂者那样需要一个动态语料库吗?你需要一个历时的语料库探寻语言变化吗?

有一些专门语料库使用很广泛。应用语言学家对第二语言学习者的书面语和口语语料库很感兴趣。这些第一语言是汉语或德语的学习者是如何说英语和写英语的？他们的发展模式是类似的还是有区别？能把水平低的学习者和水平高的学习者的语言表现进行对比吗？学习者语料库可以和本族语者语料库进行对比吗？

通常，翻译学者对两种语料库感兴趣：平行语料库和类比语料库。平行语料库通常被认为含有翻译文本，而类比语料库包含功能对等的两种或多种语言的文本。所以收集同一作者写的书的译文，可以建一个平行语料库，而收集一些关于同一话题或类似话题的原始的未被翻译的报刊文章可以建一个类比语料库。翻译学者对于在翻译过程中发现源语言对目的语的影响比较感兴趣，并且通过把平行语料库和类比语料库相结合，他们可以判断这种影响是否存在。

至此，我们已经讨论了很多关于语料库的基本问题，请试着回答下列问题：

1. 什么是语料库？
2. 语言学家如何使用语料库去探寻词义的变化，以及借用的语法后缀的变化？
3. 下列语料库的种类有什么不同？
①通用语料库和专门语料库；
②静态语料库和动态语料库；
③学习者语料库和本族语者语料库；
④平行语料库和类比语料库。
4. 什么使语料库具有代表性？
5. 是不是所有的语料库都需要很大？什么时候小语料库会有用？

课后拓展

1. Tracking language over TIME.
①Log onto TIME interface：http://corpus.byu.edu/time.
②Type "*ista" into the search box and click "frequency" what can you find from the frequency of distribution of "*ista?"
③Go over the word list, select two or three words, and click them.
④Go through the "context," How is the word used? What is the meaning of "*ista?" Can you list some examples and provide the procedures?

2. Please search the nouns that are described in BNC and COCA.
①Log onto BYU-BNC interface：http://corpus.byu.edu/bnc.
②From the menu bar, click on List.
③Type "seedy" into the search box and click "Find matching strings" or press Enter.
④Click on the word "seedy" in the results to see some of the contexts of usage. Note down some of the nouns that are modified by "seedy," for example "affair," "hotel" and "bars." Think about what these nouns have in common.

⑤To compare your results with 520 million words of current American English, go to COCA corpus at http://corpus.byu.edu/coca/ and repeat Steps 2–5. Do you find similar nouns modified by "seedy" in American English?

1. Tracking the suffix ' * ista' over TIME.

①Log onto TIME interface: http://corpus.byu.edu/time.

②Type " * ista" into the search box and click "FREQUENCY."(图1.9)

图 1.9

③Go over the word list, select two or three words, and click them.

④Go through the context and observe the results. (图1.10)

SECTION	ALL	1920s	1930s	1940s	1950s	1960s	1970s	1980s	1990s	2000s
FREQ	2771	79	209	343	735	243	195	614	221	132
WORDS (M)	100	7.6	12.7	15.5	16.8	16.1	13.6	11.4	9.7	6.4
PER MIL	27.71	10.35	16.51	22.19	43.78	15.11	14.35	53.99	22.70	20.54

图 1.10

【示范 1】

Following the instructions, let's have a look at the frequency of distribution of "*ista." It seems that among all words with the suffix "*ista" stored in TIME corpus, "Batista," "Sandinista," "Vista," and "Personista" are the words most frequently used. By going through the context of "Sandinista," it is found that the word "Sandinista" is often collocated with "guerrillas," "National Liberation Front (FSLN)," "troops" and "revolution." If we consult Collins dictionary and discover its meaning as "one of a left-wing group of revolutionaries who overthrew President Somoza in 1979 and formed a socialist coalition government." Apart from "Sandinista," "Batista" is also a frequent word. And "Batista" is often used in certain collocations such as "Sergeant Fulgencio Batista," "Colonel Fulgencio Batista," "Boss Batista" and "Strong Man Batista." Mostly, "Batista" is used as a subject, as well as an object, and it is often shown in a sentence in which the word "Cuba" also appears. The meaning of "Batista" is "the regime of Fulgencio Batista in Cuba." Based on these findings, we can conclude that the suffix "*ista" may refer to "a group of revolutionaries/leaders who advocate certain doctrines."

The frequency demonstrated that people began to use "*ista" in the 1920s, and they widely use it from the 1950s to the 1980s. Then, the frequency people use this suffix was declining.

As for the word "vista," through the word list, we discover that people tend to use this word when they predict some things will occur in the future. For instance, the fifty-sixth example "and uplifting society-breaks up the old horizon and we see through the rifts a wider vista" uses the word "vista" as the noun word to describe the prospect. Besides, we find that the noun phrase "Buena Vista" is mentioned several times. According to the search results, "Buena Vista" means "great vision" in Spanish. Therefore, this phrase always occurs in magazine.

As for the word "Peronista," it can be used to describe a group of people who definitely supports the Arabic president Perón as "Labor &; Social Welfare. One night she appeared to accept the cheers of a Peronista union members' rally. But for once, she made no speech."

As for the word "Christa," we find the word is always used as some female people's name. For example, the twenty-ninth illustrative sentence "Christa McAuliffe was the pioneer and the vibrant symbol of this amazing new era of space" shows that someone's name is Christa.

From the analysis above, we can conclude that "*ista" is a suffix that can be put in the names of some people or objects and be used to describe somebody or some groups who definitely support someone or some thoughts. For example, "Batista" is somebody's name, and "Battista" is a kind of roadster owned by Pininfarina.

In addition, Anti-Sandinista is a group that opposed the president Sandinista, who is the legendary leader of the Sandinista National Liberation Front of Nicaragua.

【示范 2】

The list is arranged in descending order of frequency of "*ista" use. And the top three most used words are "Bastia," "Sandinista," and "Vista." The frequency of use of related words is arranged by year, "*ista" was first used in the 1920s. For different words, the most frequently used year corresponds to the darkest color of the box. There were two outbreaks of "*ista" use in the 1950s and 1980s. Both have been used more than 400 times. "Bastia," as the most frequently occurred term, was most frequently used in the 1950s. And "Sandinista" in the 1980s. "*ista" is Spanish, and its usage is equivalent to the English words "*ist" and "*ismo." The following are some examples.

A. Bastia. It is a family name. So, it almost takes the form of a person's name.

Examples: a. sergeant Fulgencio Bastia.

b. Bastia was frantic because his cousin Benito had been wounded.

c. Holding most of Cuba's guns, little Generalissimo Fulgencio Bastia last week went president-making.

d. He was wanted badly by Army Chief of Staff Bastia, with whom he had a deadly personal feud.

B. Sandinista, a member of a military and political coalition holding power in Nicaragua from 1979 to 1990. Therefore, the use of term is always related to the military.

Examples: a. the Scandinista National Liberation Front

b. … will receive squatters rights in the Coco River Valley, will be guarded by 100 Sandinista polices under the Government's orders on public works in northern Nicaagua…

C. Baptista. It is used as people's last name. It means a member of a Christian Protestant Church that baptism should take part when a person is old enough to understand what it means, and not as a baby.

Examples: a. When Brazil's Joao Baptista Luzardo arrived at B. A.'s Lacroze railway station, he was met and embraced …

b. Convinced that he had a winning combination, Baptista packed his horse off to the Kentucky Derby.

c. … in his pickup for drinks with Brazil's President Joao Baptista Figueiredo, he was instrumental in arranging state visits between Figueiredo and Reagan.

D. Fashionista: a fashion designer, or a person who is always dressed in a fashionable way.

Examples: a. whose current taste for Valentino should avert barbs from E! channel fashionista Joan Rivers.

b. not even your best friends will tell you "about how you look, say fashionista inquisitors Trinny Woodall and Susannah Constantine.

E. Barista: a person who works in a coffee bar.

Examples: a. That's a grande, eh … barista! "Lewinsky saw George Stephanopoulos at Starbucks when Lewinsky did not have a bra …

F. Fascista: a person who supports fascism.

Examples: a. Mussolini to sound off to the Italian masses, wrote in his Cremona paper Regime Fascista: "Now we can speak high and loud …

b. Now the meeting of the Fascista Grand Council, which was to have taken place during the past week …

In all, we can find that the end of the word is " * ista," mostly referring to a certain type of person or denoting the person who performed the related occupation. Additionally, the suffix " * ista" is always associated with a person's name, for example, Batista, Trista, Krista, Evangelista, Arista, etc.

【示范 3】

Question 1:

1. Words with " * ista" as suffix are not used frequently.

2. Words with " * ista" as suffix were used more frequently from 1950 to 1980.

3. Words with " * ista" as suffix are used less frequently in modern times.

4. Words with " * ista" as suffix are nouns, and these nouns are generally people's first or last names, and they may also refer to a group of people or a faction.

5. In English, the suffix " * ista" is rarely used to form words, and " * ista" is more used in Spanish, Portuguese and Italian.

Question 2:

1. Battista: Battista is a given name also surname which means Baptist in Italian.

2. Chrisra: Christa is a name.

3. Batista: Batista is a Spanish or Portuguese languages surname (although in Portuguese more common in the spelling Baptista), literally meaning "batiste." It also used as middle name.

These three words are nouns, and they all refer to people's names, so these words are generally used as subjects in sentences. In addition, in the words with " * ista" as the suffix, such as Calista, Trista, Billista also refer to people's names.

【示范 4】

From frequency of distribution of " * ista," we see that " * ista" is used most frequently in the 1950s and less frequently from 1970s to 1990s compared with other time period. Batista, Sandinista, vista, Peronista and Battista are words used most frequently (more than 200 times). Batista is used 413 times in 1950s and vista is used 443 times in 1980s. (图 1.11—图 1.13)

①According to the contexts of each word, " * ista" means a member of an organization, usually with enthusiasm towards it, and this kind of words are often used with the initial letter capitalized. It's rather common in news reports, modifying nouns like regime, leader, rally, party, organization, politician, congress, member, senator etc. For example, "Sandinista" refers to a member of Sandinista National Liberation Front. ②Also, it can describe a person who supports or follows something. For example, "fashionista" refers to a person who creates or promotes high fashion, or a person who closely follows those trends. ③By the way, "vista" can also mean the visual percept of a region. ④In addition, " * ista" can be used in the name of a person of a place, with the initial letter capitalized. For instance, Boa Vista and Buena Vista are names of someplace. ⑤As for the word barista (a person who works in a coffee bar), " * ista" simply means a person who works for something. However, this word isn't used widely and there are only four examples to refer (1998—2005).

Generally speaking, " * ista" refers to a member of an organization, or a supporter with strong enthusiasm towards something. And it can also be used as a name of someone or someplace.

图 1.11

第一章　语料库使用简介

图 1.12

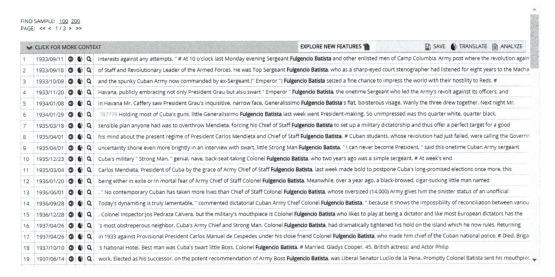

图 1.13

2. **Search the nouns which are described by the word "seedy" in BYU and COCA and compare the results.**

【示范 1】

BNC：From the results，we see that the word "seedy" modifies nouns like "affair," "hotel,""bars,""motel,""obscurity,""underworld,""motel,""prostitute,""abortionist," "prostitution,""underbelly,""nightclub,""dockside pub,""cinematic productions,""block

· 17 ·

of flats," "sub-culture," "redoubts," "sensuality," "career," "place," etc. These nouns are usually some places or behaviors that may look dirty and unpleasant, possibly connected with immoral, dishonest or illegal activities. These nouns also include some people who seem messy, sordid or disreputable. Generally speaking, "seedy" is used to describe somebody or something negative.

COCA: The word "seedy" modifies nouns like "bar," "center," "hotel," "neighborhood," "motel," "motel room," "dark side," "thoughts," "underbelly," "character," "office," "hotel," "bum," "drifter," "eyes," "incumbent," "apartment," "liquor store," "strip club," "element," "backroom," "underworld," "secret," "scam," "strip mall," "tavern," etc.

Indeed, there are similar nouns modified by "seedy" ("motel", "bar", "underbelly", "hotel" …) in British English and American English according to the results from BNC and COCA. A conclusion that "seedy" is often used to express disapproval or negative feelings towards something can be drawn from. Due to more words and longer reference period in COCA, there are much more contexts and examples to refer to in COCA compared with BNC.

【示范 2】

① The nouns that are modified by "seedy" in BNC:

room, house, bar, nightclubs, atmosphere, business, show, hotel, affair, glamour, pub, restaurant, etc.

The similarity of these nouns:

a. The majority of these nouns are notional words with a practical meaning.

b. Also, most of these nouns are material nouns that can be modified by adjectives.

c. Then, most of these nouns are words that denote a certain place, location, space, or area.

d. Most importantly, according to the meaning of the word "seedy," we can see that most of these nouns modified by "seedy" have negative meanings, such as "affair," "bar," "nightclub," "pub," and so on.

② The nouns that are modified by seedy in COCA:

thought, motel, people, bar, character, tactic, apartment, nightclub, alley, hotel, hookup, etc.

③ Similar nouns modified by "seedy" in British English:

bar, hotel, nightclub, motel, room, etc.

We can see that in both American English and British English, most of the nouns modified by the word "seedy" refer to a certain place or area. Combined with the context given, most of them refer to places that are untidy, dirty, messy, and nasty, such as "nightclub," "bar," "motel," and etc. In addition, from the retrieved list, we can see that the usage of the word "seedy" in American English is much more than that in British English, which may relate to the different language usage habits and cultures of the two countries.

【示范 3】

BNC：

seedy nightclub

seedy bar

seedy lodging-house

seedy consulting-room

seedy bed

seedy motel room

seedy atmosphere

seedy hotels

seedy restaurant

seedy image

seedy sensuality

seedy studio

After searching the word "seedy" in British National Corpus, I found, firstly, some of the nouns that go with "seedy" were nouns of places that are spatially limited.（图 1.14）Nightclub, bar, lodging-house, consulting-room, hotel, restaurant and studio are all places that are limited in space. In addition, there were a few nouns concerned with thinking that go with seedy, such as image and sensuality. The most frequent collocation is that "seedy" adds a noun expresses some limited space or a specific place or area.（图 1.15—图 1.16）

图 1.14

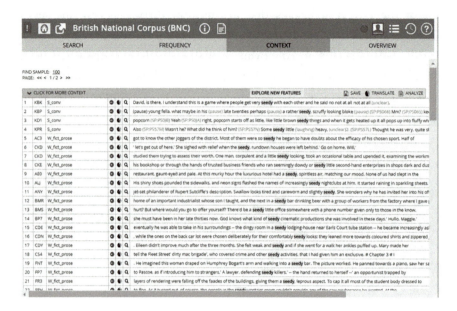

图 1.15

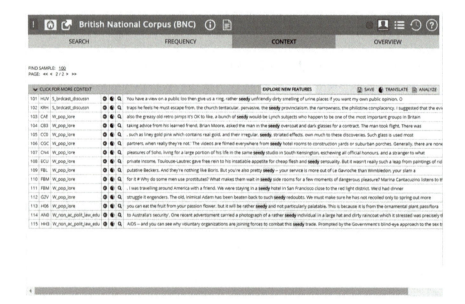

图 1.16

COCA：

seedy thoughts

seedy motel

seedy art

seedy stuff

seedy neighborhood

seedy office
seedy house
seedy apartment
seedy film
seedy underworld
seedy drifter

After searching the word "seedy" in Corpus of Contemporary American English(图 1.17), we found there were still many nouns that express places or areas collocated with "seedy." Move over, some nouns about thinking also appeared in the search results. A new discovery was that a noun denotes a person can also be matched with "seedy," such as "drifter." "Seedy" also can be matched with words that refer to a specific object such as an art painting or a film.(图 1.18)

图 1.17

图 1.18

Most of the meanings of the phrases about "seedy" the corpus showed are based on the meaning of dirty, unpleasant, and possibly connected with immoral or illegal activities. There are very few collocations of the meaning of full of seed, such as the expression of seedy cotton or seedy melon. (图1.19—图1.20)

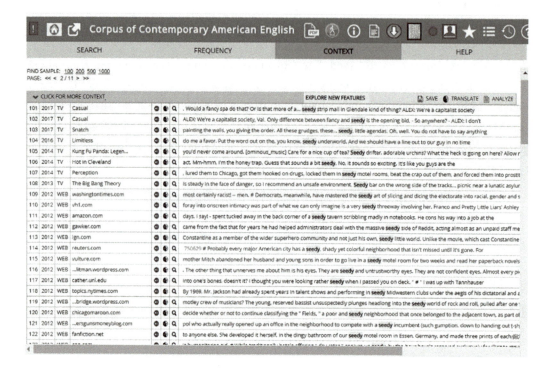

图1.19

图1.20

In conclusion, the seedy with the meaning of shabby or untidy is used more frequently than the meaning of seed.

 在线讨论

Questions of corpus design.

1. What goes into a corpus?
2. How big should the corpus be?
3. Are all corpora the same?

Answer 1: Corpus varies from one to another with nuance or big differences. Generally speaking, they are divided into different types in terms of different standards. According to the category of language, we have monolingual corpus, multilingual corpus, and comparable corpus (A corpus in a set of two or more monolingual corpora). In terms of time, we have diachronic corpus and synchronic corpus. This is not the end because there are still a lot of types according to the features. Specifically speaking, under one category the corpus still varies greatly. Taking COCA and BNC as a comparation, it is found out that their displays are different. Basically, they have different volumes. Secondly, they have different layouts and functions. COCA uses different colors to mark the parts of speech while BNC does not. BNC presents the "Collocates" in the interface and we can use the number 1, 2,… to limit the word number before and after the word we want to search.

Answer 2: ① Corpus refers to a large collection of the linguistic texts that have existed in reality. The texts may come from written materials like journals, academic papers, novels and so on, and also from spoken materials. Corpus cannot be simply regarded as a digital dictionary. It functions more powerfully. For instance, it can show us the frequency of the use of a word, and we can search strings like "*ism" to see a list of words with the suffix "-ism" and how the words are used. ② No boundary is set in the capacity of a corpus because the linguistic materials stored in the corpus will have dynamic changes and will be updated as time goes by. ③ No. Different corpus is inclined to focus on different field. Let's take the comparison of COCA and BNC as an example. The linguistic materials COCA stores are about contemporary American English, while BNC is the collection of British English. For example, we can easily find that the frequency of "seedy" in these two corpora are different and the sentences provided by COCA and BNC are also various. Also, some corpora have specific functions that other corpora do not have.

Answer 3: Corpus is composed by software tens of millions of words or even more corpus, and then you can consult the use of each word, phrase environment, frequency, collocation and so on. A corpus is a diachronic corpus. It is a corpus-based on large-scale real texts, a corpus that dynamically tracks the use of language, a corpus that monitors the development and change of language, and a "live" corpus so it has no boundary. No, there are different corpora. According to the language of the corpus, a corpus can also be divided into Monolingual, Bilingual and Multilingual. According to the unit of corpus collection, the corpus can be divided into discourse, sentence, and phrase. Bilingual and multilingual corpora can also be divided into parallel (aligned) corpora and comparative corpora according to the organizational form of corpora.

Answer 4: Corpus refers to a large collection of well-sampled and processed electronic texts, on which language studies, theoretical or applied, can be conducted with the aid of computer tools. The capacity of a corpus is not certain. Corpus is dynamic, and it is replenished dynamically. No, there are many different types of corpora, which are determined mainly by their research purpose and use. Someone once divided corpus into four types: ①Heterogeneous, ②Homogeneous, ③Systematic, ④Specialized. According to the language of the corpus, a corpus can also be divided into Monolingual, Bilingual and Multilingual. According to the unit of corpus collection, the corpus can be divided into discourse, sentence, and phrase. Therefore, not all corpora are the same.

Answer 5: In a corpus, there is the collection of words, collocations, frequency, the context of words, etc. A corpus of half a million words or more ensures that low-frequency are also adequately represented. No, every corpus has something special in word collection, frequency, etc. In BNC (British National Corpus), the collection and the context are those used in British English, while in COCA (Corpus of Contemporary American English), the collection and the context are those used in American English. Last week, we take a glance at the *TIME* Corpus, it is based on contexts from *TIME* Magazine and it is easy to see the trend of using the word. And there are some special corpora, like Coronavirus Corp.

Answer 6: Corpus is a large collection of written or spoken language stored on a computer and used to find out how language is used. It always provides us the frequency, collection and specific context of a word. A corpus needs a large principled collection of the language that has been collected from naturally occurring sources. Only after being processed, can it be available resources. It is difficult to use a specific number to describe the size of a corpus because language, the source of the corpus, cannot be measured by numbers. A great deal of language is produced by human beings every day because of the feature of creativity of language. However, a basic source of storing language is needed. I think the corpus should include the most basic and natural language we use every day. No, different corpora have different features. Firstly, the source of each corpus is different. Undoubtedly, the search results will be different. Secondly, the analysis of different corpora focuses on different aspects.

Answer 7: The corpus is a collection of written or oral materials stored on a computer to find out how a language is used. For example, COCA was collected from spoken English, novels, popular magazines, newspapers, academic texts, TV and movie subtitles, blogs and other web pages in the United States. I think there is no limit to the capacity of corpus. Language data in corpus need to be updated dynamically. No, there are different types of corpora and different classification methods. Corpus can be divided into monolingual corpus, parallel corpus, multilingual corpus and comparable corpus. These corpora are built for different purposes, so each corpus contains different information.

第二章 频 率

语料工具

- 杨百翰大学语料库(BYU)
- 苏格兰英语语料库(SCOTS corpus)

教学内容

在上一章中，我们了解了什么是语料库，语料库有哪些不同的种类，以及它们的设计、大小、是否具有代表性和一种特别的变体。此外，我们还练习了如何使用语料库来帮助我们发现单词在语境中的意义，以及如何使用语料库来了解语言的发展。

在本章中，我们将进一步了解如何使用语料库检索工具来进行频率分析。这是语料库的最基本和最强大的功能之一。统计和频率分析是定量分析的一种。英语语言研究存在两个方向，一个是实证语言学研究方向，另一个是传统的人文研究方向。前者致力寻找明晰的、可进行客观分析的实证证据，而后者更重视通过案例来获得个体独特的理解。虽然我们凭直觉认为对文本的解读是主观的，但是我们努力使其具备说服力和启发性。因此语料库语言学连接着这两个研究方向，我们对英语本质属性的论断开始得到英语研究者的支持。

语料库语言学显然属于定量研究的范畴。通过数字形式呈现并使用相关工具自动搜索文本，语料库语言学将一系列文本数据和分析工具推上台面，它们给我们提供了详细而客观的统计结果。确实，大量易获得的语言证据是语料库语言学的一大优势。然而，证据总是需要某种解读的，在讨论语料库语言学获得的定量分析结果的过程中，人文学科研究者所掌握的解释性和批评性技巧至关重要。

我们通过使用语料库及其检索工具来统计语言学特征和建构的数量，确定出现的频率和分布，最终就"语言是如何工作的"提出可靠的、概括性结论。比如说，我们对年长者和年轻人的英语对话进行录音，看看 like 这个单词出现的相对频率和分布，就能得出结论说"年轻人比老年人更频繁地使用 like 这个单词"。只要语料库建设得当，搜索工具可靠，这个结论就不易被推翻。

我们也需要注意，我们的结论"年轻人比老年人更频繁地使用 like 这个单词"并没有告诉我们这两组人如何使用 like 这个单词，也没有表明年轻人为何更频繁地使用它。对前一个问题，年轻人如何使用 like，我们可以使用更复杂的统计分析工具来找到答案。比如说，这个单词的使用是否与性别、种族甚至是否已婚等其他社会性变量相关？要解答后一个问题，为何某些年轻人更频繁地使用 like，难度更大。

因此,很多语言学家在对语料库数据进行定量分析的基础上,会增加解释性的定性分析。语料库不仅适合于定量分析,也适合于定性分析。研究者在进行定性分析时,不仅仅从语料库中得到语言使用频率和分布的信息,而且由于语料库具有快速、轻松地聚集语言材料的性能,研究者可以从中获得个案研究所需的材料。因此,一个优秀的语料库语言学家需要同时掌握定性分析和定量分析两种能力。

语料库语言学家能通过查看语料库中相关项目的频率获得大量有用信息。语言项在任何一个语料库中出现的次数叫作原始频数(raw frequency)或者观察频数(observed frequency)。我们看语料库数据时,可以区分原始频数或观察频数和标准化频率(normalised frequencies)或者相对频数(relative frequencies)。比方说,O'Keeffe,McCarthy 和 Carter 从 CANCODE(剑桥-诺丁汉英语口语语料库)和 CIC(剑桥国际语料库)中取样,他们检索的项目——第一人称代词——在口语语料数据中出现 150 989 次,但是在书面语语料数据中只出现 50 871 次。这些原始频数之所以可以进行比较,是因为两套数据库中的语料数量相同,都是五百万词。当我们比较的两个语料库的容量不相等时,比如说比较 10 亿词的 BNC 语料库和 52 亿词的 COCA 语料库时,我们就需要使用标准化频率了。标准化频率一般能告诉我们每千词,或每百万单词中出现或期望出现的次数。

下面来看几个活动。

在线练习1

1. 访问网站 http://corpus.byu.edu。
2. 选择 British National Corpus(BNC-BYU),并点击,如图 2.1 所示。

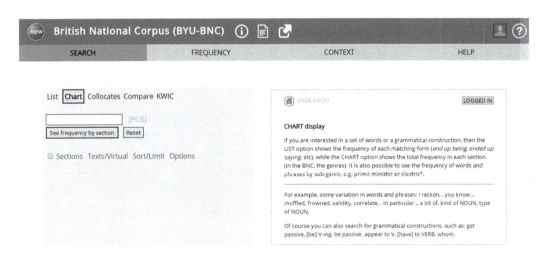

图 2.1

你的研究问题是：哪种英语变体中包含的名词比例最高？哪种英语变体中包含的名词比例最低？哪种英语变体中的名词种类最多？哪种英语变体中的名词种类最少？

当然，如果我们不研究名词，也可以研究其他词类，比方说代词 he/she, him/her, it, they/them，等等。那么，代词的分布是否与名词的分布相类似？

3. 点击 POS LIST(Part of Speech)。

4. 选择 noun. ALL。

5. 点击 SEARCH，如图 2.2 所示。

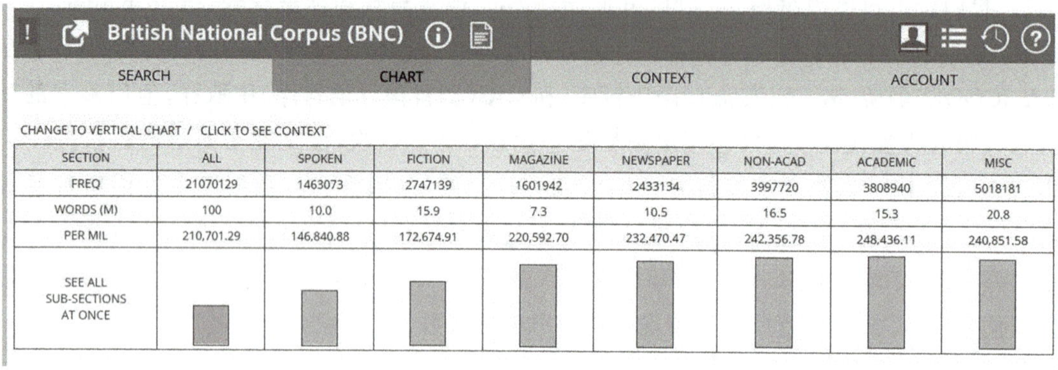

SECTION	ALL	SPOKEN	FICTION	MAGAZINE	NEWSPAPER	NON-ACAD	ACADEMIC	MISC
FREQ	21070129	1463073	2747139	1601942	2433134	3997720	3808940	5018181
WORDS (M)	100	10.0	15.9	7.3	10.5	16.5	15.3	20.8
PER MIL	210,701.29	146,840.88	172,674.91	220,592.70	232,470.47	242,356.78	248,436.11	240,851.58
SEE ALL SUB-SECTIONS AT ONCE								

图 2.2

6. 记录结果，然后重复搜寻代词。

7. 点击 POS LIST (Part of Speech)。

8. 选择 pro. ALL。

9. 点击 SEARCH，如图 2.3 所示。

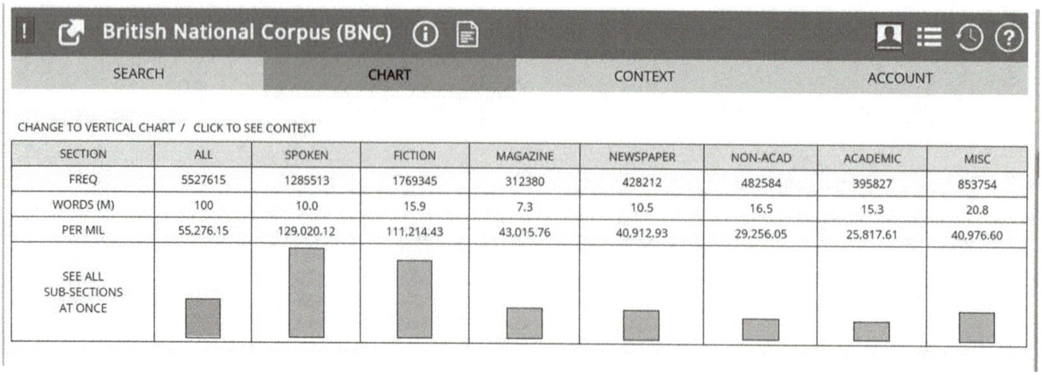

SECTION	ALL	SPOKEN	FICTION	MAGAZINE	NEWSPAPER	NON-ACAD	ACADEMIC	MISC
FREQ	5527615	1285513	1769345	312380	428212	482584	395827	853754
WORDS (M)	100	10.0	15.9	7.3	10.5	16.5	15.3	20.8
PER MIL	55,276.15	129,020.12	111,214.43	43,015.76	40,912.93	29,256.05	25,817.61	40,976.60
SEE ALL SUB-SECTIONS AT ONCE								

图 2.3

10. 记录结果。

自行检索，比较名词和代词的检索结果。

显示结果的页面会告诉你相当多有用的信息：总词汇量——形符(token)；每一个单词的数量——类符(types)；原始频率(样本中单词出现的次数)；标准频率(每百万词中出现的

次数)。你会看到屏幕上显示了口语(SPOKEN)、小说(FICTION)、杂志(MAGZINE)、报纸(NEWSPAPER)、非学术(NON-ACAD)、学术(ACADEMIC)以及杂项(MISC)等不同的英语变体。

我们从结果中可以发现英语口语中的名词出现次数最少,书面学术英语中的名词出现的频率最高。代词的特点则正好相反:代词在英语口语中出现的次数最多,而在书面学术英语中的出现频率最低。若你的判断与结果相符,那么恭喜你完成了定量分析的任务。当你问"为什么会这样?"时,你就开始了定性分析。

我们要非常小心。正如我们之前说过的,定量分析的数据本身并不提供分析。但是请思考一下我们所了解的学术英语和口头英语。前者是一种书面英语,努力将世界转换为我们能谈论和描述的东西。因此,我们期待学术英语中含有大量的名词,事实上确实如此。口头英语是"我"和"你"之间的面对面交流,此外人们经常讨论其他的男人和女人,因此口头英语中出现大量的代词时,我们并不会觉得惊讶。频率统计证实了我们对不同英语变体特征的预判。

语料库语言学的研究证明我们一直以来持有的假设,就是在某些特定项目的频率上,口语和书面语存在一些基本的差别。表2.1中可以看到最常见的前20个单词及其原始频率(分别来自CANCODE和CIC)。

表2.1 常见单词及其原始频率

No.	CANCODE spoken corpus		CIC written corpus	
	Word	Frequency	Word	Frequency
1	the	169,335	the	284,174
2	I	150,989	to	132,335
3	and	141,206	and	125,526
4	you	137,522	of	122,903
5	it	106,249	a	114,381
6	to	105,854	in	84,940
7	A	103,524	was	59,454
8	yeah	91,481	it	51,642
9	that	84,930	I	50,871
10	of	78,207	he	50,007
11	in	62,796	that	46,195
12	was	50,417	she	41,607
13	it's	47,837	for	41,606

续表

No.	CANCODE spoken corpus		CIC written corpus	
	Word	Frequency	Word	Frequency
14	know	46.601	on	38.361
15	is	45.448	her	36.500
16	mm	44.103	you	35.773
17	er	43.476	is	34.871
18	but	41.534	with	33.829
19	so	40.071	his	32.535
20	they	38.861	had	31.420

我们预期冠词 the 和 a 以及增补型连接词 and 在日常英语和书面英语中出现的频率都很高,这一点在表 2.1 中得到了验证。但是,更细致地对比一下口语和书面语中最常见的单词,我们会发现一个特殊的模式。在口语中,I 和 you 出现的频率比书面语中出现的频率要高 3 倍。口语中的高频形符还有如 yeah 及表示赞同或犹豫的 mm 和 erm,这些词在书面语中出现的频率显然没有那么高。即使是表示同意的 yes,它的出现频率也不在 CIC 的前 50 名中。动词 know 似乎在口语语料库中高频出现,进一步研究检索词来源可以发现这是因为 know 经常出现在 I know 之类的表达结构中,I know 就和 yeah 一样,用来表示赞同。频率分析表明说话者使用这些词的目的是"投射他们的自我形象,和谈话者创造良好的关系,理解并使用基本的语法和逻辑关系来加强相对低频词汇"(O'Keeffe et al.,2007)。O'Keeffe,McCarthy 和 Carter 给出了上述解释,他们就已经开始从报告频率等定量研究数据转向了更定性的办法来分析为什么词汇呈现出这样的频率。这样,他们就将关于频率的实证数据和语言学家的专业技能结合了起来。

在线练习 2

比较苏格兰英语语料库(SCOTS corpus)中 I know 在一系列书面语和口语语料中的使用频率。这个活动还告诉你如何在苏格兰英语语料库中使用高级搜索选项从而进行一个完整的搜索。以下是步骤:

1.登录 www.scottishcorpus.ac.uk。

2.点击 Advanced search(高级搜索)。

3.点击 General(综合),然后点击 Word search(单词搜索),在 Word/phrase(concordance)(关键词)一栏中键入"I know",如图 2.2 所示。

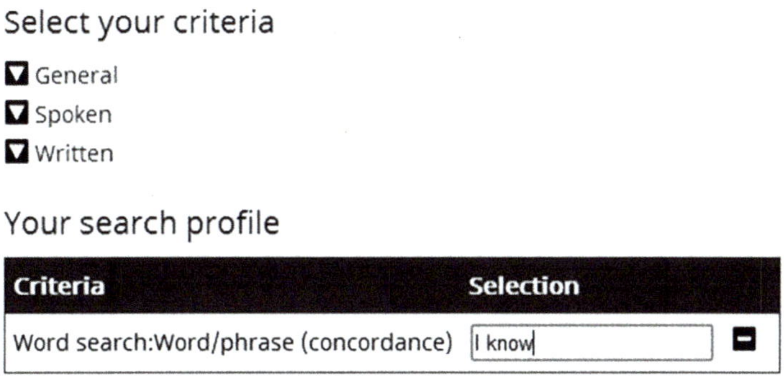

图 2.2

4. 点击 General,然后点击 Document details(文本),选择 Spoken texts(口语文本)。

5. 点击 Spoken(口语),然后点击 Audio type(音频类型),再点击 Conversation(对话),如图 2.3 所示。

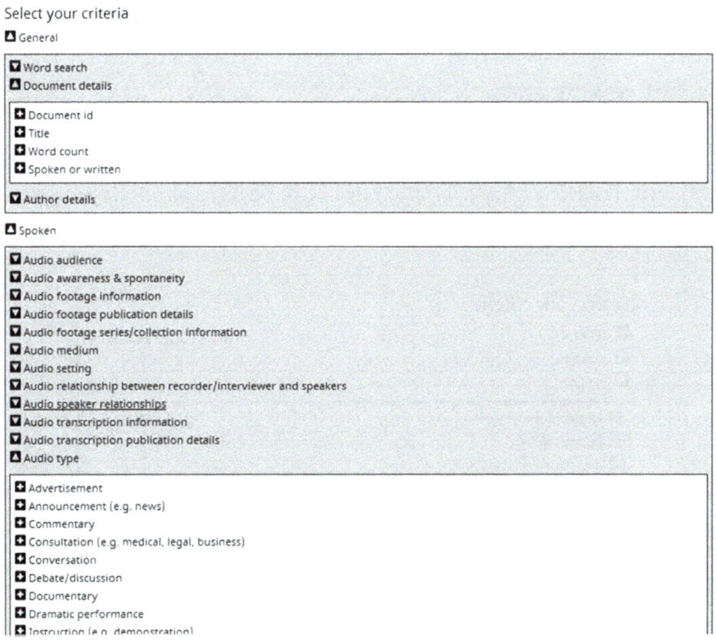

图 2.3

6. 在结果显示之后,下拉页面略过关键词,看看对话列表里使用 I know 标准化频率的情况。点击 Norm,将使用频率按标准化排序。在这个语料库里,标准化频率提供了每 1000 个词的检索项,列出了使用 I know 的最低和最高标准化频率(注意文本类型),如图 2.4 所示。

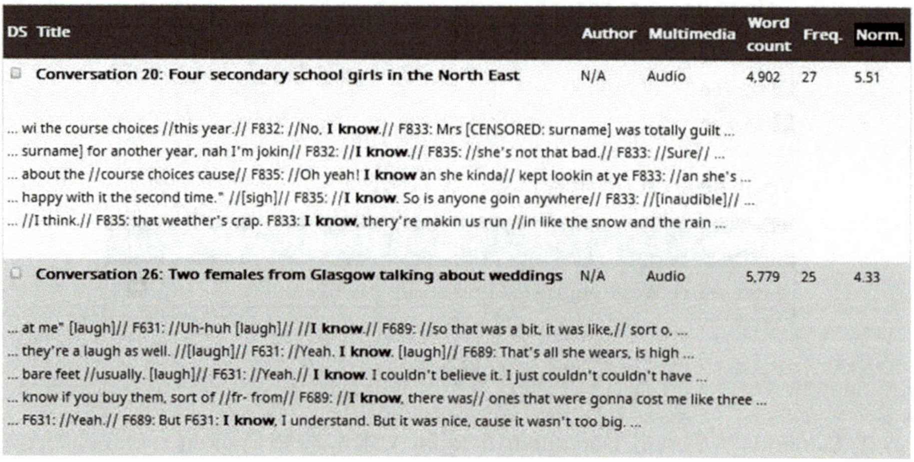

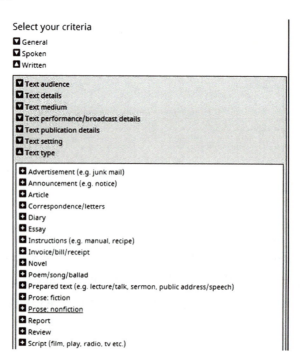

图 2.4

7. 点击高级搜索,开始另一项搜索。

8. 点击 General(综合),然后点击 Word search(单词搜索),在 Word/phrase(concordance)(关键词)一栏中键入"I know"。

9. 点击 General,然后点击 Document details(文本),选择 Written text(书面语文本)。

10. 点击 Written(书面语),点击 Text type(文本类型),选择 Prose:nonfiction(散文:非小说),如图 2.5 所示。

图 2.5

11. 当结果显示之后,下拉页面,在写作文本列表里看看使用 I know 的标准化频率。同样,标准化频率提供了每 1000 个词中使用 I know 的检索项。

12. 比较一下口语和书面语的文本搜索结果。什么类型的口语文本中使用 I know 的频率低,什么类型的口语文本中使用 I know 的频率高?什么类型的书面语文本中使用 I know 的频率低,什么类型的书面语文本中使用 I know 的频率高?返回去看看 I know 关键词列表中低频率和高频率使用的具体情况。这个短语的使用真的有助于说话者或作者与其听众或读者之间的关系处理吗?如果可以,它是怎么起作用的呢?

完成这项任务后再继续。

在中学女生的对话中 I know 的使用频率最高,其标准化频率值为 5.51(以在每 1 000 个词中出现的次数计算),在 BBC 采访一个 20 世纪 60 年代男士的对话中 I know 的使用频率最低,其标准化频率值为 0.08(以在每 1 000 个词中出现的次数计算)。在写作文本里,使用 I know 的最高频率为 7.41,最低频率为 0.02。尽管 I know 使用的高频率出现在短诗歌里,但总的来说 I know 在口语中使用的频率高于在书面语中使用的频率。I know 在苏格兰英语语料库书面语文本中使用频率很低;排在第二的使用频率为 3.69,在这之后就开始减少了。对比之后,我们会发现书面语中原始频率和口语中的 25 个文本一样高,接下来的标准化频率是 4.33 和 3.71。很明显,说话人在口语中使用 I know 的频率很高。为什么会这样呢?

有一点是清楚的,即 I know 在口语里出现的频率高于书面语。要进一步探究它的功能,需要看看原始频率和标准化频率。下面是苏格兰英语语料库里在口语中使用 I know 的例文:

> F835:But I mean and then he was like, you know like you're sayin that north east Scotland's like the highest drug use and everythin, it's only like eleven percent or somethin//isn't it//
>
> F832://I know, yeah// but that's what he waspointin out to us tha-that it wasn't as bad as it was// made out to be.//
>
> F832://I know.//
>
> F835:eleven percento Scotland they should be //praisin
>
> F833://What about//
>
> F835://the eighty-nine percent or whatever it is//
>
> F832://I know, but I think// //folk just conc-[laugh] folk just//
>
> F835://[laugh]I know! //

通过对真实文本的检测,我们可以使用定性研究来解释 I know 为什么在口语中使用频率很高。通过这个具体例子,我们会发现:

I know 表明同意说话人的意见。

I know 增强了交际双方的共同点。

I know 还作为①引起话轮转换的标记语,②渠道返回的标记。换句话说,它表明你现在可能想说,或者你仅仅是在听。

这些功能真的对交际有帮助,使得说话人之间的关系保持良好。定性研究和定量研究的数据都具有启发性。

本章主要关注频率分析,但是你还可以尝试回答以下问题:

解释定量和定性分析的差别;

解释原始频率和标准化频率的差别;

解释为什么使用标准化频率很重要;

搜索一些关于词性和具体表达的语料;

把定性和定量分析结合起来解释你的发现。

在 *Exploring English with Online Corpora*(Anderson et al.,2017)的第二章里,你可以读到更多关于频率分析的内容。

课后拓展

TASK:Compare written and spoken language.

This activity compares the frequency of use of "I know" in a set of written and spoken documents in BYU-BNC corpus through CHART.

What kind of spoken documents have a low/high frequency of instances of "I know?" What kind of written documents have a low/high frequency of instances of the same phrase? Go back and look in detail at a concordance list of "I know" in the documents that show low and high frequencies of use. Does the use of this phrase really "help to manage relations" between speaker/writer and audience? If so, how?

典例示范

【示范 1】

Generally speaking, "I know" is much more frequently used in spoken language compared with written language. Compared with spoken language, written language is more formal and less casual. The normalised frequency of total spoken documents is 900.67 while that of any kinds of written documents is far lower, with the highest normalised frequency of 396.87 in fictions.

In spoken documents, conversation (normalised frequency=1614.22) has the highest frequency of instances of "I know." What's more, this phrase is also often used in consultation (normalised frequency=753.69), classroom (normalised frequency=555.32), meetings (normalised frequency=577.80) and interviews (normalised frequency of market research interview＝537.29；normalised frequency of oral history interview ＝ 390.50). However, according to BNC corpus, it's never used in sermons, speech scripts, tutorial, broadcast disc and lectures; and "I know" is hardly used in nature science, broadcast documents, law lectures, sports live, and broadcast news. From what is found in the corpus, people use "I know" to express their opinions and feelings, like in the phrase "as far as I know," or to interact with others in a conversation to show their approval and they are listening, or share one's own experience. Usually, pronouns are used in bilateral communications, along with some verbs like believe, know, think, etc. Undoubtfully, these help to manage relations between speaker and listeners by making them feel more involved. However, on some formal occasions, like lectures, sermons, and courts, people speak in an objective way and avoid using "I know" with the help of rules, regulations, facts, principles etc.

In written documents, fiction (normalised frequency＝396.87) has the highest frequency, especially in prose and drama, while academic works (normalised frequency＝14.94) have the lowest frequency. When we have a closer look at those documents, we can see that academic works (normalised frequency＝14.94) and non-academic works (normalised frequency＝31.04) like engineering, natural science, medicine, laws, and arts seldom use the phrase "I know." Fictions, which tell stories or express strong feelings, aim to make connections with readers for resonance, so "I know" helps close the gap between them. This phrase makes readers feel they are really on the scene. As for academic works or non-academic works, writers try to explain or elucidate truth, theories, facts, or principles, and they needn't build emotional bonds with readers, thus hardly using "I know."

To sum up,"I know" can help shorten the distance between the speaker/listener and audience and convey certain feelings, through building bridges between them, making them feel closer to each other.

【示范 2】

In spoken language,"I know" is used most frequently in conversation, because the language used in daily conversation is more colloquial. And "I know" rarely appears in spoken English types such as l_sci, b_doc, l_law and l_com. The low usage rate of "I know" in these texts is because the language should be official under these occasions so the colloquial language is seldom used.

In written language,"I know" appears most frequently in fictions, including drama, poetry and prose. This may because there are many dialogues in them and more expressions of the author's own feelings, so the subjective expression of "I know" is used more frequently. In contrast, its usage rate in academic, newspaper and magazine are low, which is because their language is more formal, so it is necessary to reduce colloquial expression.

The usage of "I know" helps to manage the relations between the speaker/writer and audience to a certain extent. In daily oral communication, it is a colloquial expression, which indicates that the listener has grasped the speaker's meaning. In writing, it appears in the form of object clauses, which expresses some feelings and thoughts of the speaker. Therefore, the use of "I know" between the speaker/writer and the audience helps to manage their relations.

In spoken documents, the "conversation" takes up the high frequency—6477 while "l_sci" is only 2 frequency which is the low one. In written documents, this phrase appears highly in "Fiction" with 6314 frequencies while rarely in "Academic" with 229 frequencies.

"I know" can help to manage relations in a spoken context but not in a written academic context. Firstly, it can bring the speaker closer to the audience while the speaker presents a vocative speech. For example, this context "I mean I'm speaking as a resident of The Stow and I know there's lots of complaints and shopkeepers and er people in the flats" reflects the speaker trying to comfort the audience so that the speaker admits the existence of complaints which is apparently revealed in that situation. Besides, during the conversation, the appearance of "I know" is a relatively positive response to the audience by making the audience know that their interaction is relatively efficient. In this context, "Well it's a different, you know different department. Mm, I know yes. And this was, this, that, that wouldn't entered," the addressee responded to the addresser that "I know that which department wouldn't entered." Obviously, this phrase is frequently used in a spoken context especially in conversation. As for written documents, although fiction takes up a large frequency, this phrase actually appears in the form of a conversation among characters so that to some extent we can consider it as conversation document. In fiction, the characters' relationship is usually revealed by their conversation. The author makes use of this phrase to bring readers into the setting that has occupied in the fiction. However, academic documents only take up 229 frequencies in written documents, because its focus isn't the relation with the audience but is to objectively present the research to its audience.

【示范3】

By searching on BNC corpus, we have found that when people are communicating with others in the daily life, they prefer to say "I know" to keep the conversation going smoothly and state the information they have known. It has the highest frequency of instances of "I know."（图2.6）What's more, in consult, meeting, classroom and interview, these spoken documents also have high frequency of instances of "I know." However, in sermon, tutorial and broadcast_disc, people never say "I know."（图2.7—图2.8）

图 2.6

SECTION	ALL	SPOKEN	FICTION	MAGAZINE	NEWSPAPER	NON-ACAD	ACADEMIC	MISC
FREQ	18614	8974	6314	596	705	512	229	1284
WORDS (M)	100	10.0	15.9	7.3	10.5	16.5	15.3	20.8
PER MIL	186.14	900.67	396.87	82.07	67.36	31.04	14.94	61.63

图 2.6

图 2.7

SECTION	ALL	SPOKEN	FICTION	MAGAZINE	NEWSPAPER	NON-ACAD	ACADEMIC	MISC
FREQ	448	293	21	42	60	27	5	0
WORDS (M)	100	10.0	15.9	7.3	10.5	16.5	15.3	20.8
PER MIL	4.48	29.41	1.32	5.78	5.73	1.64	0.33	0.00

	advert	essay_schl	email	misc	instruction	essay_univ	let_pers	religion	hansard	admin	inst_doc	biog	commerce	let_prof
	10	15	49	398	5	0	20	94	261	0	2	383	0	0
	0.5	0.1	0.2	9.1	0.4	0.1	0.1	1.1	1.1	0.2	0.5	3.5	3.7	0.1
	18.19	103.42	233.54	43.86	11.52	0.00	385.80	84.33	227.01	0.00	3.69	109.60	0.00	0.00

图 2.7

图 2.8

SECTION	ALL	SPOKEN	FICTION	MAGAZINE	NEWSPAPER	NON-ACAD	ACADEMIC	MISC
FREQ	448	293	21	42	60	27	5	0
WORDS (M)	100	10.0	15.9	7.3	10.5	16.5	15.3	20.8
PER MIL	4.48	29.41	1.32	5.78	5.73	1.64	0.33	0.00

	l_sci	mtg	b_doc	court	interv2	consult	l_law	class	b_news	dmnstr	l_soc	sports	parl	conv	l_com	interv1	debate	l_arts	speech-	misc	b_disc	tutor
	2	771	8	20	312	99	6	229	29	6	45	6	21	6477	0	64	61	13	210	194	0	0
	0.0	1.3	0.0	0.1	0.8	0.1	0.0	0.4	0.3	0.0	0.2	0.0	0.1	4.0	0.0	0.3	0.3	0.0	0.4	0.4	0.7	0.1
	90.22	577.80	197.27	159.44	390.50	753.69	120.54	555.32	114.01	196.72	290.85	186.90	220.99	1,614.22	0.00	537.29	219.06	261.26	467.90	477.01	0.00	0.00

图 2.8

Besides, in written documents, in the fictions, such as drama and prose, have a high frequency of the instances of "I know." (图 2.9) In the commerce, the essay of university, the administration and so on, people never write "I know." I think the reason may be that these circumstances are more formal, and "I know" is too causal, so that it never occurs.

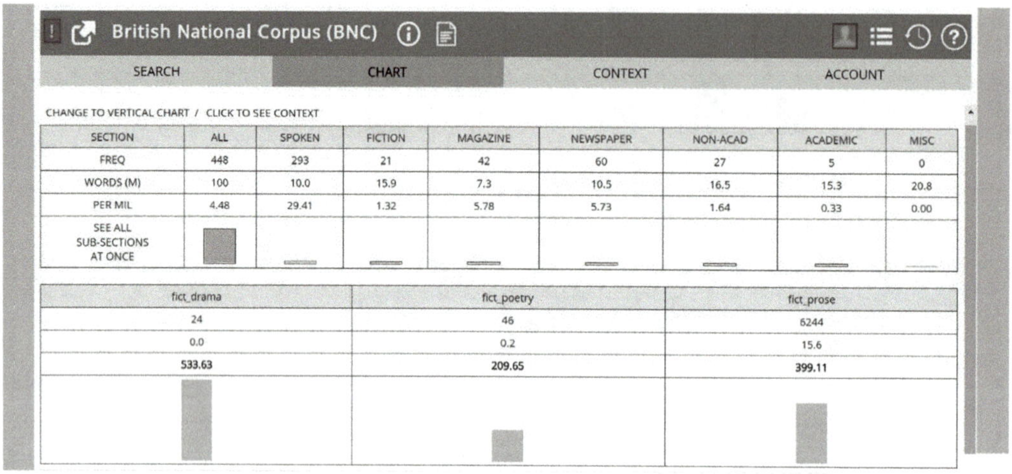

图 2.9

Of course yes, this phrase is helpful for managing relations' between speaker or writer and audience. (图 2.10—图 2.11) Firstly, it is a positive phrase when we are chatting. For instance, "I mean I know there not everybody's cup of tea, but I mean they way." In spoken English, we use "I know" to agree on other's opinion, and then pose our ideas in a polite way lest the person you are talking with feel awkward and offended. Then, "I know" also appears in a repetitive way, for example, "I know, I know!" The intention of speaker is to comfort the listener, and then talk with he when he is in clam.

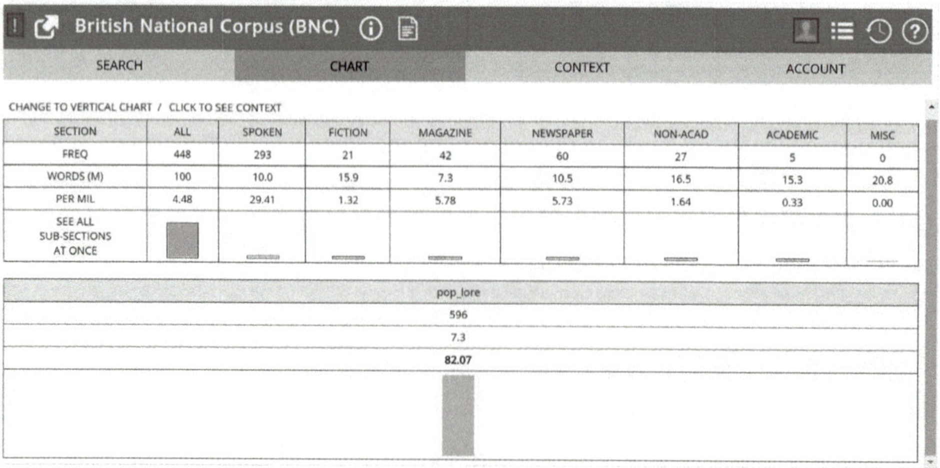

图 2.10

SECTION	ALL	SPOKEN	FICTION	MAGAZINE	NEWSPAPER	NON-ACAD	ACADEMIC	MISC
FREQ	448	293	21	42	60	27	5	0
WORDS (M)	100	10.0	15.9	7.3	10.5	16.5	15.3	20.8
PER MIL	4.48	29.41	1.32	5.78	5.73	1.64	0.33	0.00

tabloid	sci_o	sci_b	misc_b	rprt_b	sports_b	arts_b	soc_o	new_arts1	editrl_b	rprt_o	comrcl_o	soc_b	comrcl_b	sports_o	script_b
102	2	3	55	8	15	9	111	23	11	132	13	9	4	170	38
0.7	0.1	0.1	1.0	0.7	0.3	0.2	1.1	0.3	0.1	2.7	0.4	0.1	0.4	1.0	1.3
142.95	36.81	46.42	53.93	12.20	51.22	38.21	98.64	66.50	109.28	49.22	31.92	111.16	9.61	168.34	30.10

图 2.11

【示范 4】

About SPOKEN documents:

conv has a high frequency of 1614.22 per million.(图 2.8)

I_com, b_disc, tutor, speech + and sermon have low frequency of 0.00 per million. (I_com owns both 0 frequency and 0.0 words(M))

About WRITTEN documents:

fict_drama of FICTION has a high frequency of 533.63 per million.(图 2.9)

engineering of ACADEMIC, essay_univ, admin, commerce and let_prof of MISC have a low frequency of 0.00 per million. (essay_univ and let_prof both have 0 frequency and 0.1 words(M))

When one speaker says "I know" in a conversation, it will indicate that this speaker gets some ideas from others who just said something. As an audience, we can get to know that the speaker who just said "I know" would like to show his/her attitude toward the former information or give out his/her statement which is possibly related to the former information. In this way, the use of such a phrase will help the audience catch the speaker's attitudes toward something or some new statements of his/her.

There are two typical sentences in the context. One is "You are a little jealous rogue; I know you are." The writer here used "I know" to emphasize the former information "You are a little jealous rogue" which had already been put out to the audience directly or implicitly. The other one is "I know Pamela has your good word." In this sentence, the writer showed the audience some new information or restated the previous information from the character's perspective by giving a declarative phrase. In this way, the writer will emphasize some necessary information or just state new information with the use of this phrase to help the audience better understand the drama plot.

Of all the spoken documents of "I know", we can see that this phrase is used most frequently in conversation, with the number of 1614.22. (图 2.8) Similarly, this phrase is also frequently used in meeting, consult, class, and interview. However, among the spoken documents of I_com, b_disc, tutor, speech, and sermon which are very formal and regular, the phrase "I know" has the lowest frequency of use, with the number of 0.

Of all the written documents, the phrase "I know" is used most frequently in fiction. Under the category of fiction, this phrase is used more frequent in drama and prose. Non-academic and academic in written documents are the two categories with the lowest frequency of using this phrase, which is owing to their formal style.

By observing the concordance list of high andlow-frequency usage of the phrase "I know," we conclude that this phrase has a helpful and positive effect on managing relations between the speaker/writer and the audience. "I know" is frequently used in the conversation of spoken documents, because it can help the speaker better convey a certain meaning or emotion, increase the sense of interaction and also help the speaker to build a closer relationship with the audience by making the spoken expression more casual, coherent and authentic. For example, in "joined up themselves (SP:PS002). No, that's true Alan, no, aha, I know, aha, and they want to pay somebody a fee to do a service," "I know" phrase plays a role of better expressing the speaker's current emotion and making the conversation more fluent and native, thus narrowing the distance between the audience and the speaker.

在线讨论

Why do we neednormalised frequency?

Answer 1: Normalised frequency refers to number of items that appears in a corpus per thousand or per million words. I think there are 2 reasons for people to use normalised frequency in corpura.

In the corpus, we can know the frequency of a certain type of words per thousand or per million words by normalised frequency. We can compare the normalised frequency of this kind of word with the normalised frequency of other kinds of words. So, we can find the tendency of people to use a certain type of words in this corpus. For example, in the BNC corpus, people use nouns more frequently than pronouns per million words. When we analyze the reasons, we will find that nouns are used frequently in people's language because nouns' function is to describe things, so people often use them in daily life because there are lots of things closely related to our lives. The normalised frequency of pronouns is relatively less, because in a context, a noun must be mentioned first and then there will be a corresponding pronoun.

In addition, we can also analyze the language habits of people in the corpus by comparing thenormalised frequency of the same type of words in different corpora. In addition to the corpus comparison between languages, it is also possible to compare the normalised frequency of the same type of words in different language corpora. Then We can explore the differences in the usage habits of the same type of words in different languages. We can also explore the normalised frequency of one word in every thousand or every million words in the corpus. Then, we could investigate why the frequency of the word is high or low. This is also an exploration of people's habit of using words. For example, in the spoken language corpus, the standardized frequency of the word "I" appears very high. I think it is because in daily conversations, people are more inclined to express their opinions.

Answer 2: When corpus-based studies examine the frequency of an element across texts, it is critical to make sure that the counts are comparable. Normalised frequency (relative frequency), a way to adjust raw frequency (total times of an item appears in a corpus), refers to the number of times an item appears in a corpus per thousand/million words. This method enables us to compare two corpora of different size. For example, when we analyze the frequency of nouns appeared in fictions and magazines and BNC corpus shows that the raw frequency is 2 747 139 and 1 601 942 respectively, it may occur to us those nouns are more frequently used in fictions because of the lager number of words. The whole size of fiction and magazines, however, is 15.9 million words and 7.3 million words respectively, therefore, the normalised frequency can be obtained: 172 776.04 (2 747 139/15.9) nouns per million words and 219 444.11 (1 601 942/7.3) nouns per million words. To be more precise, nouns are used more frequently in magazines than fictions. Notably, the raw frequency is likely to mislead us to a wrong conclusion as it doesn't accurately reflect the relative frequencies in each corpus. Applying normalised frequency makes individual corpus be comparable even if the corpora consist of different quantities of texts or speeches.

Answer 3: Usually, the frequency will be reported in the results of corpus retrieval and glossary generation. We can compare different frequencies by grouping them into a common base. For example, what does it mean that "many" occurs 100 times in a corpus? The word appears 105 times in the other corpus. Could it be said that "many" is more commonly used in the second corpus? Obviously, just because 105 is greater than 100 does not mean that many is more commonly used in the second corpus. It is easy to imagine here that the two corpora may not be the same size. In the usual way of thinking, we can calculate the percentage of "many" in the two corpora, so that we can compare them. In this case, the frequency of "many" in the two corpora is reduced to a common base of 100, that is, how many "many" appear in every 100 words.

Answer 4: The frequency obtained by percentage here is a standardized frequency. In some literature, the standardized frequency is also called the normalised frequency or the nominal frequency, that is, the frequency based on a unified benchmark. In-text collection, text or conversation constitutes the final corpus sample. These samples are obtained by means of certain sampling methods. In the study, we need to describe the occurrence and distribution of these samples. In addition, we often need to observe the probability of co-occurrence between different language items in a given context and to see how much variation a language item(s) presents between different texts. The actual observed frequency of a search term Raw Frequency divided by the total frequency (usually the total number of words in the text or database) to determine how many times the search term appears in each word.

Answer 5: First of all, we could figure out this question by starting with an easy question. What is normalised frequency? Normalization means to have a measure for something in the same, fixed, easy to use range. So normalised frequency means to set your sampling frequency to 1, and other frequencies are expressed as a percentage of it. Sometimes the frequency range is very wide, which makes it inconvenient to use. After normalization, it is converted to [0,1]. So, the reason why we need normalised frequency is that the number of times an item appears in a corpus is beneficial to compare the distribution of various frequencies. In this way, a unified standard is unified, we could also analyze data very conveniently. Another advantage of normalised frequency is to prevent overflow of data.

Answer 6: Normalised frequency refers to the number of times an item appears in a corpus per million or per thousand words. The reason why we need normalised frequency is that the normalised frequency can make sure that the counts are comparable. If we use a percentage of the whole corpus to represent the frequency of a word, for example, there are 1103 examples of the word "Lancaster" in the written section of the corpus, the BNC's writing section contains 87 903 571 words of running texts, meaning that the word "Lancaster" represents 0.013% of the total data in the written section of corpus, but the texts in a corpus are not the same length, then frequency counts from those texts are not directly comparable, therefore, the percentage may not convey meaningfully the frequency of the word. A common solution to this problem is to convert each frequency into a value per million words, per thousand words, this is the normalised frequency, "normalization" is a way to adjust raw frequency counts from different lengths so that they can be compared accurately.

Answer 7: Frequency is very important to corpus research. In corpus related research, the comparison is often implemented in the frequency comparison. The comparison of words or phrases within a corpus and the comparison between two or more corpora is often the frequency comparison. For example, which word "man" or "woman" is used more in the same corpus? In corpus-based research, we often compare the frequency of one or some words, phrases or other language units in two corpora by chi square test or other statistical methods, so as to determine whether there are significant differences in the use of specific language units between the two corpora.

Answer 8: The normalised frequency is to set the sampling frequency to 1, and other frequencies are expressed as a percentage of it. Sometimes the frequency range will be very large, and it will be very inconvenient to use. After normalization, it will be converted to [0,1]. In this way, a unified standard is realized, which is helpful to compare the distribution of each frequency. Another purpose of normalization is to prevent data overflow. Frequency is very important to corpus research. In corpus related research, the comparison is often implemented in the frequency comparison. The comparison of words or phrases within a corpus and the comparison between two or more corpora is often the frequency comparison. For example, which word "man" or "woman" is used more in the same corpus?

第三章　关键词索引

📘 语料工具

- 杨百翰大学语料库(BYU)
- 当代美国英语语料库(COCA)

👤 教学内容

上一章我们讲了词频以及如何解释词频。本章我们使用一个更普遍、更强大的搜索程序：索引工具。

在这一部分我们将会考虑下列问题：

- 什么是语境中的关键词；
- 分析关键词索引行；
- 人工处理大数据。

本章涉及的活动和例子出自苏珊·亨斯顿(Susan Hunston)所著的《应用语言学中的语料库》(*Corpora in Applied Linguistics*)一书中的第三章。

什么是关键词索引检索？关键词索引是一个搜索词或短语语料并将语料库中所有包含这个词或短语的例子找出来置中并显示前后语境的程序。这个中心词或搜索项通常为节点，有时被叫做语境中的关键词。

关键词索引的美妙在于我们可以把包含某个词或短语的例子放到一起，看看这些在非常有限的语境里的例子。即使在有限的语境里，词或短语的用法结构和意义对于实践分析也是很清楚的。

词汇索引检索阐明了一个问题，即一个词或短语的本义或比喻义是否是其典型用法。我们可以通过 Susan Hunston 所举的例子 recipe 来解释这个问题。

如果你在标准词典里查找 recipe 这个词，例如牛津高阶英语词典，你会看到两种解释（见图 3.1）：第一种是字面意思或者叫本意，意为烹饪说明，包括所需原料菜单；第二种解释是比喻义，意为可能会造成某事。哪一种意思是真正典型的意思，哪种意思在语料库中出现的频率更高，在词典里无法找到答案。关键词索引将帮助我们回答这些问题。

第三章 关键词索引

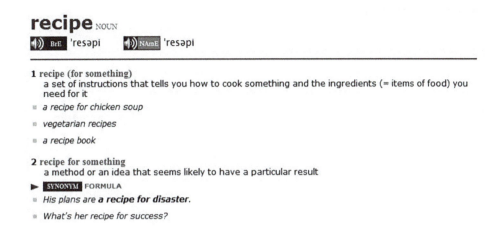

图 3.1

在线练习 1

要探究前面这些问题,我们可以在杨百翰大学语料库(BYU)中进行检索,也可登录当代美语语料库(COCA)。我们可以选择语境中的关键词检索并选择按字母顺序排列检索结果。输入 recipe 并点击 Keyword in Context(KWIC)(语境中的关键词),如图 3.2 所示。

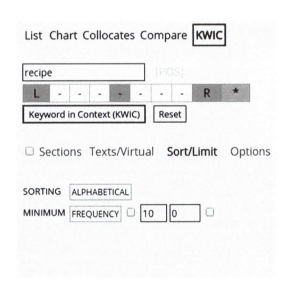

图 3.2

我们可以得到图 3.3 所示的结果。

图 3.3

正如我们看到的，目前的结果（这些结果可能会随着语料库的扩大而发生变化）有很多都和 recipe 这个词的字面意思有关，即烹饪说明。然而，如果我们将包含 recipe for 例子的列表下拉，模式就发生了变化，如图 3.4 所示。我们看看检索到的例子，如 recipe for honey seed mustard dressing（蜂蜜籽芥末酱配方）、recipe for breath-taking growth（导致惊人增长）或 recipe for gridlock stagnation（导致僵局，停滞）。

图 3.4

尤其是当我们把介词 for 放在 recipe 后面，可以区别这个词的本义（烹饪）和比喻义（可能会造成某事）（比喻义比较典型）。本义和比喻义的检索结果显示在同一页上，可能是褒义也可能是贬义，贬义用红色标出。

我们试图通过这个例子来探究一个更广泛的问题，即我们凭直觉认为的一个词的本义是不是这个词的典型用法？就像我们看到的，recipe 这个词的本义非常普遍，但是比喻义也非常典型（尤其是 recipe 后面跟 for 时）。

在我们定义词语或讲授词语用法时，要注意词语的典型用法和本义一样重要，还要注意这些词特定表达的语法特点及意义。

有一个问题：当我们开始手动处理超过 5 亿 2000 万个词（这是目前 COCA 的规模）的语料库时，会有数以千计的常用词汇和短语要处理。如何才能处理这么庞大的数据？

语料库语言学的前辈约翰·辛克莱（John Sinclair）认为，当我们处理庞大的词汇数据时，操作应如下：

①看看前 30 个关键词索引行并注意结构；
②看看下一个 30 行并注意是否有新结构；
③一直往下看，直到没有新结构出现。

John Sinclair 把这个方法叫作意义转换，它非常好用。我们可以把这个方法稍做调整用来解决我们的问题。

Susan Huston 优化了 Sinclair 的方法，她提出假设检验的方法：

①小规模检索关键词索引行并寻找结构；
②进一步检索来检验假设并给出新假设；
③一直往下看，直到没有新假设需要验证。

在线练习 2

我们可以用"转换法"或"假设检验法"来分析 Hunston 的另外一个例子：在澳门大学常见的一个词 suggestion。

点击 KWIC 关键词检索并选择按字母顺序排序检索结果，如图 3.5 所示。

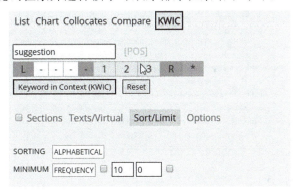

图 3.5

下拉列表，看看前 30 个关键词检索行和出现的结构，然后继续下拉列表，看看下一个 30 行有没有新结构出现，持续进行，直到没有新结构出现，如图 3.6 所示。

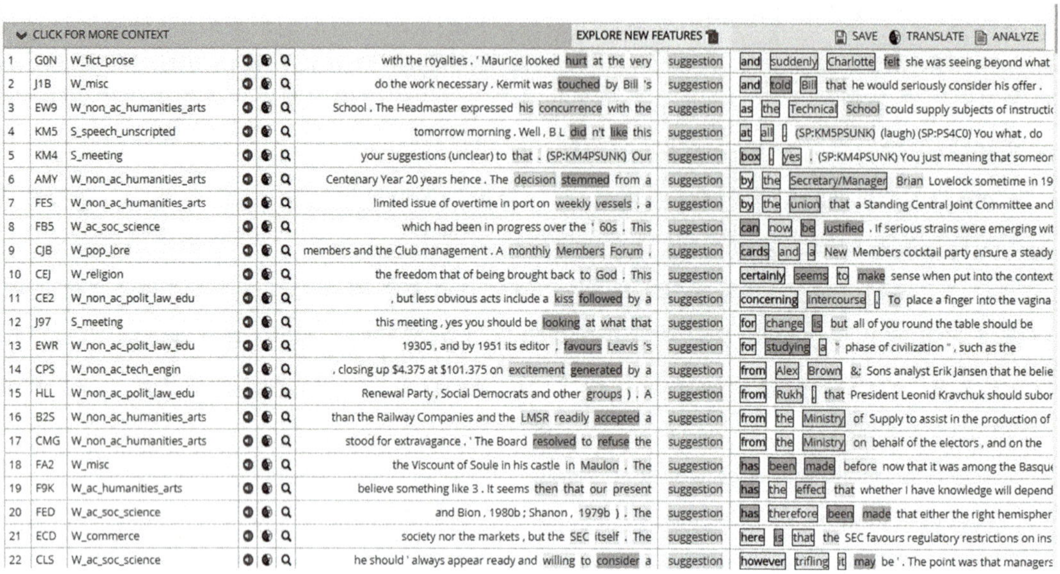

CLICK FOR MORE CONTEXT | EXPLORE NEW FEATURES | SAVE | TRANSLATE | ANALYZE

1	G0N	W_fict_prose	with the royalties . ' Maurice looked hurt at the very	suggestion	and suddenly Charlotte felt she was seeing beyond what
2	J1B	W_misc	do the work necessary . Kermit was touched by Bill 's	suggestion	and told Bill that he would seriously consider his offer .
3	EW9	W_non_ac_humanities_arts	School . The Headmaster expressed his concurrence with the	suggestion	as the Technical School could supply subjects of instructi
4	KM5	S_speech_unscripted	tomorrow morning . Well , B L did n't like this	suggestion	at all (SP:KM5PSUNK) (laugh) (SP:PS4C0) You what , do
5	KM4	S_meeting	your suggestions (unclear) to that . (SP:KM4PSUNK) Our	suggestion	box yes . (SP:KM4PSUNK) You just meaning that someor
6	AMY	W_non_ac_humanities_arts	Centenary Year 20 years hence . The decision stemmed from a	suggestion	by the Secretary/Manager Brian Lovelock sometime in 19
7	FES	W_non_ac_humanities_arts	limited issue of overtime in port on weekly vessels , a	suggestion	by the union that a Standing Central Joint Committee and
8	FB5	W_ac_soc_science	which had been in progress over the ' 60s . This	suggestion	can now be justified . If serious strains were emerging wit
9	CJB	W_pop_lore	members and the Club management . A monthly Members Forum ,	suggestion	cards and a New Members cocktail party ensure a steady
10	CEJ	W_religion	the freedom that of being brought back to God . This	suggestion	certainly seems to make sense when put into the context
11	CE2	W_non_ac_polit_law_edu	, but less obvious acts include a kiss followed by a	suggestion	concerning intercourse To place a finger into the vagina
12	J97	S_meeting	this meeting , yes you should be looking at what that	suggestion	for change is but all of you round the table should be
13	EWR	W_non_ac_polit_law_edu	19305 , and by 1951 its editor , favours Leavis 's	suggestion	for studying a " phase of civilization " , such as the
14	CPS	W_non_ac_tech_engin	, closing up $4.375 at $101.375 on excitement generated by a	suggestion	from Alex Brown &: Sons analyst Erik Jansen that he belie
15	HLL	W_non_ac_polit_law_edu	Renewal Party , Social Democrats and other groups) . A	suggestion	from Rukh that President Leonid Kravchuk should subor
16	B2S	W_non_ac_humanities_arts	than the Railway Companies and the LMSR readily accepted a	suggestion	from the Ministry of Supply to assist in the production of
17	CMG	W_non_ac_humanities_arts	stood for extravagance . ' The Board resolved to refuse the	suggestion	from the Ministry on behalf of the electors , and on the
18	FA2	W_misc	the Viscount of Soule in his castle in Maulon . The	suggestion	has been made before now that it was among the Basque
19	F9K	W_ac_humanities_arts	believe something like 3 . It seems then that our present	suggestion	has the effect that whether I have knowledge will depend
20	FED	W_ac_soc_science	and Bion , 1980b ; Shanon , 1979b) . The	suggestion	has therefore been made that either the right hemispher
21	ECD	W_commerce	society nor the markets , but the SEC itself . The	suggestion	here is that the SEC favours regulatory restrictions on ins
22	CLS	W_ac_soc_science	he should ' always appear ready and willing to consider a	suggestion	however trifling it may be ' . The point was that managers

图 3.6

大概在 200 行以后，频率最高的结构是 suggestion 后面总是出现 that，频率最低的结构为 suggestion 和 for、to 连用。我们再来具体看看这些结构，重新检索一遍，这次的检索项为 suggestion that 或 suggest for。这会带来一些特别的结构。

看看 suggestion that 的检索结果，可以发现，“that-短语”通常用来限定 suggestion。

再看看 suggestion with，就会发现检索的结果没什么用，如图 3.7 所示。在很多检索结果里，“with-短语”不和 suggestion 连用，但和其他短语连用成为一个大短语的一部分，例如 he responded to the suggestion with something 中的 respond… with，这个搜索结果可以排除掉，因为它跟我们要研究的 suggestion 不相关。

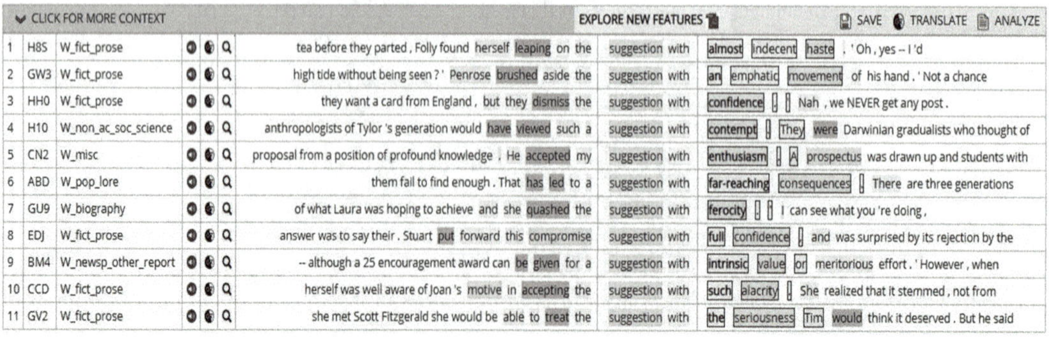

CLICK FOR MORE CONTEXT | EXPLORE NEW FEATURES | SAVE | TRANSLATE | ANALYZE

1	H8S	W_fict_prose	tea before they parted , Folly found herself leaping on the	suggestion with	almost indecent haste . ' Oh , yes -- I 'd
2	GW3	W_fict_prose	high tide without being seen ? ' Penrose brushed aside the	suggestion with	an emphatic movement of his hand . ' Not a chance
3	HH0	W_fict_prose	they want a card from England , but they dismiss the	suggestion with	confidence Nah , we NEVER get any post .
4	H10	W_non_ac_soc_science	anthropologists of Tylor 's generation would have viewed such a	suggestion with	contempt They were Darwinian gradualists who thought of
5	CN2	W_misc	proposal from a position of profound knowledge . He accepted my	suggestion with	enthusiasm A prospectus was drawn up and students with
6	ABD	W_pop_lore	them fail to find enough . That has led to a	suggestion with	far-reaching consequences There are three generations
7	GU9	W_biography	of what Laura was hoping to achieve and she quashed the	suggestion with	ferocity I can see what you 're doing ,
8	EDJ	W_fict_prose	answer was to say their . Stuart put forward this compromise	suggestion with	full confidence and was surprised by its rejection by the
9	BM4	W_newsp_other_report	-- although a 25 encouragement award can be given for a	suggestion with	intrinsic value or meritorious effort . ' However , when
10	CCD	W_fict_prose	herself was well aware of Joan 's motive in accepting the	suggestion with	such alacrity She realized that it stemmed , not from
11	GV2	W_fict_prose	she met Scott Fitzgerald she would be able to treat the	suggestion with	the seriousness Tim would think it deserved . But he said

图 3.7

我们也可以再深入一点，在检索 suggestion to 时添加词性限制，如图 3.8 所示，在 POS 一栏中选择 verb.INF。

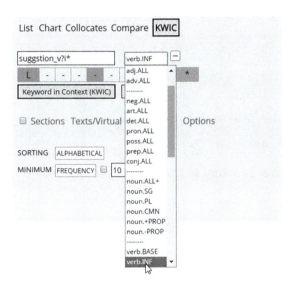

图 3.8

我们会得到所有跟 suggestion to 搭配的动词，如图 3.9 所示。

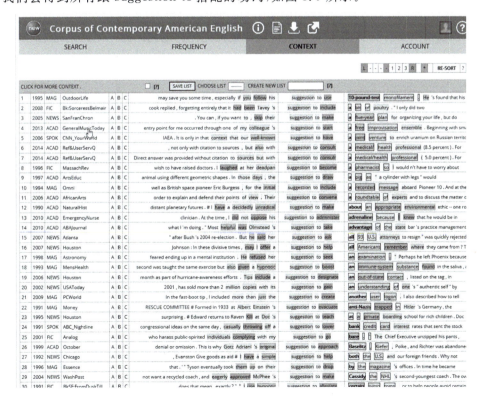

图 3.9

需要注意的是，每个人的检索结果都可能会有所不同，因为 COCA 是一个动态语料库，会随着时间的推移而更新。

即便如此，所显示的结果也足以表明这种结构模式的意义。来看一些例子：

- our well-known suggestion to have a joint venture
- the suggestion to put Scott in charge
- Kathy's Day 1 suggestion to push incremental sales
- a modest suggestion to read the Bible
- my suggestion to use the seat belt

在这些例子中，to＋VP 的结构解释了 suggestion 的内容，这是一种典型用法，但是也有例外，例如：

- He call me at Mr. Foster's suggestion to tell me that an accounting firm had been engaged
- They used innuendo and suggestion to fan the flames of a tense racial environment

这些结构的意义有点不同，用来表达建议的目的，即 in order to tell me(为了告诉我)，in order to fan the flames(为了煽动情绪)。

像 suggestion as to 这样相对不太常见的结构呢？这里我们做一个特别检索，如图 3.10 所示，检索一个一眼就能看出是不同的典型结构。你能发现吗？

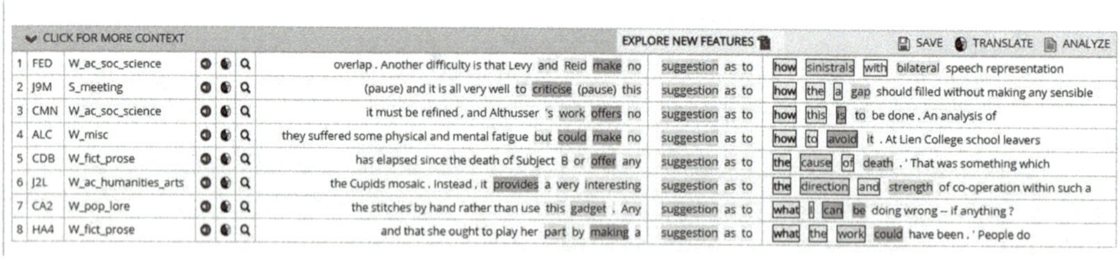

CLICK FOR MORE CONTEXT				EXPLORE NEW FEATURES	SAVE TRANSLATE ANALYZE	
1	FED	W_ac_soc_science	overlap . Another difficulty is that Levy and Reid make no	suggestion as to	how sinistrals with bilateral speech representation	
2	J9M	S_meeting	(pause) and it is all very well to criticise (pause) this	suggestion as to	how the a gap should filled without making any sensible	
3	CMN	W_ac_soc_science	it must be refined , and Althusser 's work offers no	suggestion as to	how this is to be done . An analysis of	
4	ALC	W_misc	they suffered some physical and mental fatigue but could make no	suggestion as to	how to avoid it . At Lien College school leavers	
5	CDB	W_fict_prose	has elapsed since the death of Subject B or offer any	suggestion as to	the cause of death . ' That was something which	
6	J2L	W_ac_humanities_arts	the Cupids mosaic . Instead , it provides a very interesting	suggestion as to	the direction and strength of co-operation within such a	
7	CA2	W_pop_lore	the stitches by hand rather than use this gadget . Any	suggestion as to	what I can be doing wrong -- if anything ?	
8	HA4	W_fict_prose	and that she ought to play her part by making a	suggestion as to	what the work could have been . ' People do	

图 3.10

相对不太常见的结构，如 suggestion as to 后面跟着问句，比如 how、which、where 加上情态动词，例如 suggestion as to how I should wear them。

简而言之，手动转换大约 200 个含有 suggestion 的例子，其结构变化说明 suggestion：

①经常作为独立名词；

②经常和 that 引导的限定从句连用，用来限定 suggestion；

③有时和 to 引导的非限定性从句连用，用来解释 suggestion 或表达目的、建议；

④有时后面跟随介词 of/for；

⑤几乎不跟复合介词 as to 连用,如果连用,则后面跟着疑问词＋情态动词,表达可能性或责任。

总之,关键词索引检索对于人工分析词汇和短语来说是一个非常有用的工具。即使在有限的语境中,比如一个关键词前后只有 4 个或 5 个词,仍旧可以反映出这个词有哪些典型用法(字面意义或比喻义)。我们可以看到意义是随着词汇和短语在特定语法结构中的使用而发生变化的,比如 recipe for 更多用在比喻语境中。词汇索引也有局限性,即使我们使用了转换和假设检测的方法,也可能会错过特定的结构。此外,有时需要弄明白更多检索项涉及的语境的意义或结构。在后面的章节中,我们将探索克服这些局限性的方法。

本章中我们谈到了这几个方面:

①关键词检索行的性质;

②中心意义和典型用法的区别;

③转换法和假设检验法在检索词汇时的过程。

所有语料库语言学家都在尝试分析关键词检索行,请你自己选择一些词和短语,看看它们在语料库中的结构吧。

课后拓展

Please explore the usage of "suggestion" and answer the following two questions by COCA.

1. What is the normal function of the "to ＋ verb phrase?"
2. What is the meaning of the "to ＋ VP" in these lines？(图 3.11)

In Pacific Gas & Electric , the Court moved from a	suggestion	to a clear statement : listeners ' rights are subordinated to
question : " Where 's Daddy ? " There was his	suggestion	to a couple trying to get pregnant : The quickest way would
this wont be enough , at this point youll get a	suggestion	to buy the linear accelerator and the synchrotron booster . now
conducted , and that alone has altered figures . # The	suggestion	to disband the youth division is " one of the most misplaced
. That will solve the problem very simply SUNUNU Your	suggestion	to eliminate the PAC 's sounds like what the Republicans have
for the positive answer . Goldberg (1998) provides one	suggestion	to enable the patient to retain a sense of worth and personhood
's Soviet Union (13) . And thus Gaddis 's	suggestion	to explain Stalin 's course from allegedly abandoned world
Jiang Zemin , Cboe was reported to have accepted the Chinese	suggestion	to freeze North Korea 's nuclear program . Cboe , however ,
cheerier topic , I 've decided to take Mark Spittle 's	suggestion	to heart and become a Beltway Bandit . How could I have
, who are now suing Microsoft over the ordeal . Our	suggestion	to Microsoft : ship out 16GB microSD cards to make up for
to do with his Cujo scenario once it 's escalated from	suggestion	to noisy mayhem . The buildup portion of the evening is much
when it comes to discussing the auto-industry and Mr. Romney 's	suggestion	to take the car companies through bankruptcy ? # A system of
vote against any politician who voted for it . # My	suggestion	to the AJC is to publish the names of the members of

图 3.11

1. What is the normal function of the "to + verb phrase?"

By using COCA to have a better understanding of the word "suggestion," we can find the following results. Different examples are presented when changing the minimal frequency. The following illustrations are based on the examples from COCA.

According to my findings, "to + verb phrase" is mostly used as attribute which explains the preceding noun, and it's like an adjective. That being said, "to + verb phrase" means the same thing as the noun it modifies. It is a kind of postnominal modifier, which shows appositive relations. Here is an example: Edward returns to Raven Kill at Doc's suggestion to teach at a private boarding school for rich children. "To teach at a private boarding school" is what the "suggestion" is exactly about, and it explains the "suggestion."

Sometimes, "to + verb phrase" normally can be used to express a purpose. For instance, in the sentence "the point of the article was meant as a suggestion to open up your options," "to open up your options" is the purpose of the "suggestion."

To sum up, "to + verb phrase" helps make the modified nouns easier to understand by explaining the detailed information about it. "To + verb phrase" usually shares the same meaning with modified nouns, but it goes further in details and is more specific. Normally, there are six functions of the "to + VP."

Firstly, it can serve as the subject.

e. g., It is important to plan for our study.

Secondly, it can serve as the predicative.

e. g., Anyhow, my goal is to provide humans with a life of high quality.

Thirdly, it is the infinitive as object.

e. g., People began to wonder how long the disaster would last.

Fourthly, it can serve as the attribute.

e. g., He was the last one to leave school yesterday.

Fifthly, it can serve as the object complement.

e. g., He asked me to give a speech to the class.

Sixthly, it can serve as the adverbial.

e. g., He wept to hear the news.

2. What is the meaning of the "to + VP" in these lines?

If it is the Noun before "to + VP," there are three relations.

Firstly, it is the "subject-verb" relationship. For example, she was the last student to arrive (who arrived).

Secondly, it is the "verb-object" relationship. For example, this is the best book to read (that we can read).

Thirdly, it is the appositive relationship. For example, actually, I have no wish to quarrel with you.

In these lines, "suggestion to do" is the infinitive as object. For example, in the sentence "The suggestion to disband the youth division is one of the…," "to disband the youth division" to the specific explanation of "the suggestion." Therefore, it is the infinitive as object. Here, the suggestion and "to disband the youth division" are both about the same thing. Therefore, they are the appositive relationship.

1. The use of "suggestion:" suggestion for; suggestion that; suggestion from; suggestion of; suggestion to.

2. The "to + verb phrase" usually indicates the purpose or result.

3. For example:

①I want to make a suggestion to prove how many people have found jobs.

In this sentence, the "to + verb phrase" means purpose.

②It was my suggestion to bring her back in.

In this sentence, the "to + verb phrase" means result.

在线讨论

Why is concordance useful? In what way?

Answer 1: Concordance is an index that lists the key words in a book or work in alphabetical order. It helps language learners locate words in context. And it brings a lot of convenience to researchers. They can improve the efficiency of collecting information.

Answer 2: Concordance provides users with information about where in the text each word occurs and how often it occurs. In other words, it shows typical uses of certain words, which are sometimes different from its central meanings. It reveals to the readers the common usage of the word and how to use it naturally.

Answer 3: A concordance is a data structure used by the database storage to quickly find specific data. Keyword index is usually compiled by computer, which is relatively simple, fast and greatly reduces the number of filtrating. Therefore, it can speed up searching.

Answer 4: Because concordance can not only list the context of relevant content for researcher to analyze, but also count the frequency of keywords appearing in the text and give quantified parameters to the analysis. Therefore, prime concordance function is a very important part of corpus. Keywords play an important role, because through keywords in context, learners can understand the context in which keywords are used, their typical collocations, semantic features and so on.

Answer 5: Concordance is an alphabetical list of all the words used in a book or set of books, with information about where they can be found and usually about how they are used. Thus, it can help us easily and quickly find where is the key word in contents and information about its usage. In linguistics study, it assists to locate all the words in an assembled corpus with their linguistics context and frequency. For example, KWIC frequently is applied to testify whether a word is frequently used.

Answer 6: Concordance is an alphabetical index, and it has a variety of search options. Researcher can use concordance to find words, phrases, tags and text types in the context in a form of a concordance. Generally speaking, concordance provides us not only the literal meaning of the words, but also the metaphorical meaning. And it helps us have a comprehensive understanding of the usage of the word.

Answer 7: The concordance is an alphabetical index of the principal words in a book or the works of an author with their immediate contexts. It is also a list of occurrences of words from the corpus. The most common concordance type is KWIC (keyword in context). It can help readers to find key words or phrases, and the usage and collocations quickly in corpus. It provides the overall meaning, so that we can better understand how the word or the phrase is used. This will help us to use English more accurately.

Answer 8: A concordance is a program that searches a corpus for a word or phrase and presents those expressions (or a sample of them) amidst a number of words that come before and after, the central word is sometimes called the node. Sometimes called a Key Word in Context (KWIC) program. A concordance is a data structure used by the database storage to quickly find specific data. Keyword index is usually compiled by computer, which is relatively simple, fast and greatly reduces the number of filtrating.

Answer 9: Concordance is a structured record of keywords assigned to different files or to different locations within a file. The most common concordance type is KWIC (keyword in context). The results of the study are color-coded. Therefore, it brings a lot of convenience to researchers. It provides not only the literal meaning of the words or phrases being queried, but also their metaphorical meaning. This will help students understand English better and use idiomatic English more accurately.

第四章　词语搭配

语料工具

- 英国国家语料库(British National Corpus)
- 杨百翰大学语料库(BYU)
- 当代美国英语语料库(COCA)

教学内容

本章尝试使用另外一个强大的检索程序——词语搭配(也就是一些特定的表达有规律地出现在词和短语的语境中)。

简要回顾一下,在前三章中,我们解答了以下问题:什么是语料库?为什么语言学家觉得语料库很有用?如何在语料库中检索特定的词和短语的使用频率?怎样分析频率数据?第三章讲了词汇索引检索,这可以让我们在即时语境中看到这些单词和短语并可以人工检索他们的用法,还讲了用转换法和假设检验法来处理庞大的词汇索引数据,以及如何分析这些原始数据。我们也已经熟悉了一些在线语料库,比如 BNC、COCA、TIME 等。

这一章来看看什么是词语搭配,如何测量它,如何检索搭配成分,以及如何分析搭配数据。

首先解答一个问题,什么是词语搭配?简单地说,搭配是用数据测量词或短语共同出现在文本里的概率的强度。通常借助词汇索引行,我们可以探讨 4~5 个词范围内的任意检索项或节点的词语共现。下面来看看用数据的方法测量词语共现的可能性。有很多不同的方法,而且也不仅仅是讨论词语共现的频率。在语料库中,词语搭配不仅是共现的频率,在讲搭配的时候,应该把频率考虑在内。在某种程度上,我们依靠直觉判定哪些词和短语在特定语境中有可能共现。例如在说英语的群体当中,大多数人都知道哪些词会和 fish 或 student 共同出现,你希望在这些词附近找到那些词吗?

我们可以用 BYU-BNC 来探索这个问题。

在线练习1

在菜单栏里选择 Collocates(搭配),键入 fish,如图 4.1 所示。节点任意一边的单词数设置为 4,在这个跨度内检索。通常检索节点前后各四个词,也可以调整为只检索节点前后各一个词。也可以把感兴趣的词性具体化,但此时暂时先空着。检索频率结果,但是要把结果限定在搭配测量—交互信息—3,这个问题做详述。最基本的是交互信息值 3+,指这些词语共现的可能性是有意义的,3 以下则意味着偶尔出现。交互信息值越高,检索项共现的可能性越大。点击 Find collocates,如图 4.1 所示。

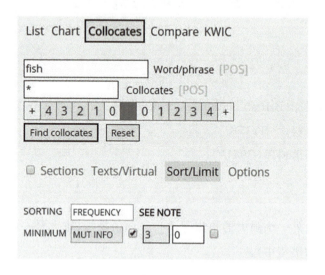

图 4.1

SEE CONTEXT: CLICK ON WORD OR SELECT WORDS + [CONTEXT] [HELP...]

		CONTEXT	FREQ	MI
1		CHIPS	265	
2		FISH	264	
3		MEAT	161	
4		SPECIES	143	
5		TANK	129	
6		CAUGHT	125	
7		SHOP	111	
8		CHIP	109	
9		CATCH	100	
10		FRESH	99	
11		EAT	98	
12		FEED	96	
13		SEA	93	
14		STOCKS	78	
15		BIRDS	77	

图 4.2

频率检索结果(图 4.2)令人惊讶。一般英国人都知道 chips 是最常见的搭配,就像 fish and chips。在语料库里共现的词语有 265 个,MI(交互信息)值高达 7.8。看看搜索结果,就能发现 fish 常跟 fish、meat、spices、tank 等词语共同出现,其交互信息值浮动不大:spices 的交互信息值为 4.79;tank 为 5.46,但是频率却很低。这意味着什么?这说明 spices 和 tank 都和 fish 搭配,但是 tank 和 fish 共现的可能性更高。就像交互信息值一样,在分析词语搭配时,频率共现和数据测量都很有用。

我们可以把词语搭配分析看作是一个更严格、更优秀的词汇索引分析版本。除了手动检索不同的索引行,比如把 student 作为节点,看看它在语境中的表现,检索程序搜索所有的语料库并计算出它的频率和词语共现的可能性。词语搭配分析是对词汇分析的有益补充。

在线练习 2

下面来看看 student 的词语搭配,同样在 BNC(图 4.3)和 COCA(图 4.4)中进行频率检索。

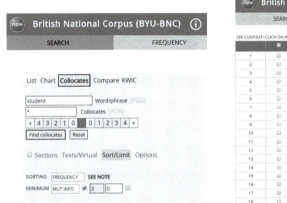

图 4.3

图 4.4

如同我们所料想的,student 这个词在这两个语料库中显示的搭配词语是相近的,university、college、teacher、learning、graduate 等都是 student 的惯用搭配。在 BNC 的检索结果中 Oxford 是一个很显眼的词;并且,只有在英式英语中 grants 才是一个有意义的惯用搭配,而与之相对应的 loans 在两个语料库里都有。词语搭配暗示文化差异,medical 和 nurse

在英式英语语料库中有出现,但在美式英语语料库中缺失,这可能是语料库的设计导致的。

回顾一下,词语搭配是一种数据测量,由语料库自动计算得出。和手动分析词汇索引行相比,它更客观、更全面。测量词语搭配时,程序可以搜索每一个节点前后 4 个词。节点可以是具体的词形或词目(包括检索相关词形),如 singular + plural。用杨百翰大学语料库检索词目时,需要在检索项上打上方括号。

在线练习 3

检索词目[terror](图 4.5),结果会显示单数名词的搭配和复数名词的搭配。BNC 语料库中的检索结果显示,常与[terror]搭配的词有 reign、fear 和 sheer 等(图 4.6)。

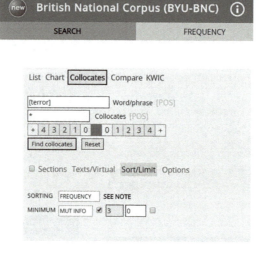

图 4.5

HELP			FREQ	ALL	%	MI
1		REIGN	54	1835	2.94	7.86
2		FEAR	25	8883	0.28	4.48
3		SHEER	22	1997	1.10	6.45
4		CAMPAIGN	19	9170	0.21	4.04
5		FLED	18	1267	1.42	6.81
6		LOYALIST	13	477	2.73	7.75
7		TERROR	12	1397	0.86	6.09
8		SCREAMED	11	971	1.13	6.49
9		GRIPPED	10	649	1.54	6.93
10		SCREAMING	10	1326	0.75	5.90
11		PAIN	10	6985	0.14	3.50
12		IRA	9	1688	0.53	5.40
13		PURE	9	3384	0.27	4.40
14		SPREAD	9	6067	0.15	3.55
15		BALANCE	9	8668	0.10	3.04
16		TACTICS	8	1371	0.58	5.53
17		TUNNEL	8	2253	0.36	4.81
18		SUDDEN	8	4083	0.20	3.96
19		STRIKES	7	1654	0.42	5.07
20		ABSOLUTE	7	3379	0.21	4.04
21		STRUCK	7	3975	0.18	3.80
22		FILLED	7	4963	0.14	3.48
23		AGONY	6	899	0.67	5.72
24		HEARTS	6	1450	0.41	5.03

图 4.6

搭配检索的结果表明 reign 和 sheer 是惯用搭配,其交互信息值很高(可能是因为常用表达 reign of terror 和 sheer terror);而 fear 虽也是惯用搭配,但是人工检索值比较低,可能是因为没有和 terror 结合成一个公式化的短语,还可能是因为跟 fear 搭配共现的词有很多。例如,在 COCA 中 sheer fright 仅出现了两次,而 sheer terror 出现了 90 次。

那么,词语搭配告诉我们什么?告诉我们意义的结构。在 BNC 中,terror 的惯用搭配是 loyalist 和 IRA(爱尔兰共和军)。

词语搭配是一个数据测量,可以用不同的方法计算,因为不同的语料库和文本分析程序使用了不同的测量方法,所以我们有必要了解这些方法。计算搭配的主要方法有 MI(人工检索)值、t 值、z 值。

所有的计算都会问两个问题:在给定范围内能找到多少该节点搭配的例子?(观察值)有多少该范围内的搭配,鉴于搭配频率在语料库中是一个整体?(期待值)

此外,计算概率的方法也不同。

我们来看 t 值的计算。

①从观察值里减去期待值,结果被标准差除(也就是给定阈值中的节点共现率和形符数量)。很明显,如果阈值大小改变,t 值就会变化。

②t 值为 2 或更高时,通常被认为有意义。

计算交互信息值时,同样要考虑观察值和期待值。

③比较实际词语共现和所期待的词语搭配(如果语料库中的词随机出现)。

④交互信息值为 3 或更高,则被认为是有意义的。

z 值基于观察值和期待值的不同。

⑤比较观察值和期待值,从频率的平均值中算出标准差。

⑥z 值越高,搭配强度越高。

这里要强调的是,搭配可以用不同的公式计算。那么使用哪一种方法来计算,重要吗?答案是肯定的。因为计算的本质就是要确定概率,每种方法都有其优势和劣势。BYU 语料库倾向于使用交互信息值,因为交互信息值不会受限于语料库的大小,这样,就可以在不同的语料库之间进行比较,比如 BNC、COCA、COHA(美国近现代英语语料库)。不同大小的语料库比较时不能使用 t 值[有些文本分析程序会计算 t 值,但是如果要比较的多个语料库的大小不同,那就要看看词语搭配的排序(从高到低),但是不能比较它们的 t 值]。

t 值趋向于包括更多语法词(冠词、介词、连词、代词),而交互信息值和 z 值会淡化常用语法词的重要性。

在线练习 4

BYU 语料库用的是交互信息值。下面来看看交互信息值。进入 TIME 语料库,检索[terror],步骤如下(图 4.7):

1. 访问 http://corpus. byu. edu;
2. 选择 TIME;
3. 点击 Collocates;
4. 键入[terror];
5. 在 Collocates 框中选择(*);
6. 把阈值设为 4 和 4;
7. 检索频率;
8. 将交互信息值设为 3。

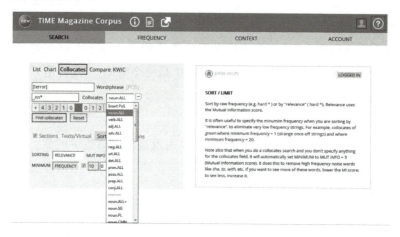

图 4.7

结果包含了很多信息,包括频率和所有的交互信息值(图 4.8)。点击其中的一个搭配,可以看到其所在语境。正如你看到的,reign of terror 是一个常用搭配,它的变体是 reign of red terror。需要注意的是,这些例子都是 20 世纪 20 年代的(在俄国十月革命后不久),如图 4.9 所示。

	CONTEXT	ALL	1920s	1930s	1940s	1950s	1960s	1970s	1980s	1990s	2000s	ALL	%	MI
1	REIGN	183	11	16	25	28	30	25	26	18	4	1400	13.07	9.03
2	CAMPAIGN	67		2	3	5	18	18	11	5	5	27580	0.24	3.28
3	PITY	45	2		4	5	13	12	1	7	1	1155	3.90	7.29
4	ATTACKS	42			1		5	2	3	1	30	6465	0.65	4.70
5	BALANCE	37				3	11	4	10	8	1	6392	0.58	4.54

图 4.8

1	1923/09/03	A	B	C	the criminal syndicalism law of California. The Wobblies would start a " reign of terror. " The members would invade the city, fill the jails, start a
2	1924/02/18	A	B	C	The Cheka's attempt to repress opposition will be accompanied by a new reign of terror in Russia, but it is too late. The seed of discontent is sown
3	1924/04/14	A	B	C	M. Titulesco, Rumanian minister to London. The incident inaugurated an anti-Semitic reign of terror that lasted in Bucharest until several regiments of troops had been called out to
4	1924/12/29	A	B	C	opposition newspapers carried similar headlines. They announced the imminence of a Reign of Red Terror. # Premier Herriot, confined to his bed by illness, read these headlines

图 4.9

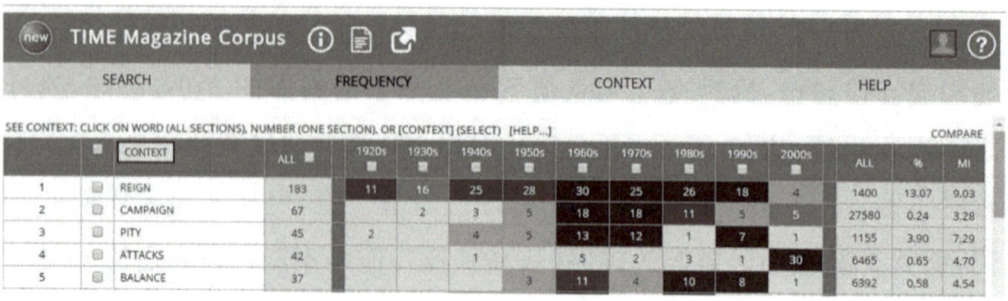

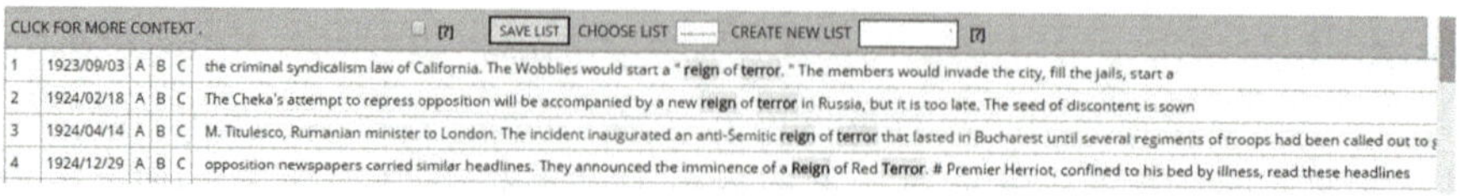

到目前为止，我们已经检索了词语搭配的频率和交互信息值(都设定在 3 或超过 3，因此都有意义，见图 4.10)从高到低发生的变化。交互信息值保持在 3+，也是可以检索的(这会告诉我们这些表达共享一个最高的共现概率，不管它们频率是高还是低)。

如果用 TIME 语料库来检索，会发现一系列古怪的短语，例如 Afghan-trained，交互信息值非常高，如图 4.11 所示。为什么这些奇怪的搭配没有出现在之前的检索结果中?

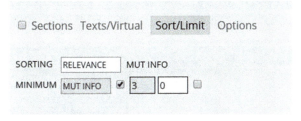

图 4.10

		CONTEXT	ALL	1920s	1930s	1940s	1950s	1960s	1970s	1980s	1990s	2000s	ALL	%	MI
1		-MORTAL	2		2								2	100.00	11.97
2		SOFIA-THIS	2			2							2	100.00	11.97
3		8/29	1									1	1	100.00	11.97
4		90S-HEIGHT	1	1									1	100.00	11.97
5		AFGHAN-TRAINED	1									1	1	100.00	11.97

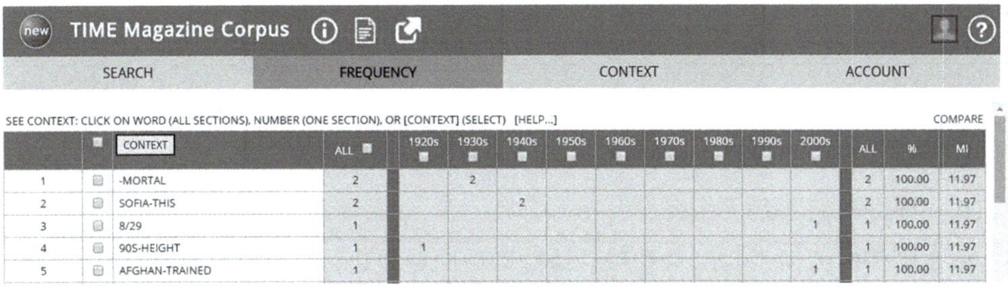

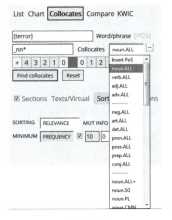

图 4.11

Afghan-trained 出现在语料库中总紧跟着 terror，其交互信息值很高，到达 12.6。然而，Afghan-trained 在 1 亿个词中仅出现了一次，所以它在 terror 这个词附近出现的交互信息值会如此之高就不奇怪了。除非我们知道一个短语在语料库中出现的真正频率，否则我们很可能会被发现的东西误导。我们可以把 Afghan-trained 的高交互信息值和低共现率与 reign 的高交互信息值和 reign of terror 的高共现率作比较。由于这个原因，在用交互信息值进行数据检索时，我们希望能够设定最小共现率。换句话说，我们需要可以筛选出那些出现少于 5 次的检索项。

可以用两种更有效的方法再次检索 terror。我们可以通过 POS 菜单选择只检索名词共现，还可以只检索在语料库中出现 10 次或 0 次以上的那些短语(图 4.12)。

图 4.12

这样做之后，更有意思的结果出现了：regin 还是很重要，但是我们找到了比 Afghan-trained 更有用的表达，那就是 pity、torture、tactics。（见图 4.13。要记得这是美国期刊语料库 1920 至 2000 年间的内容，在"9·11"事件之后，war on terror 可能会改变共现结构。）

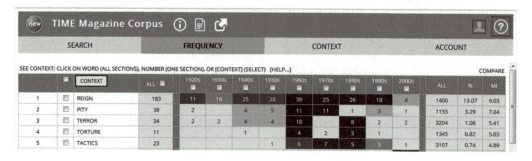

图 4.13

所以检索结果会受语料库的本质、语料搜集时期的影响，但是我们还是可以发现标准语言的一般性质。那些共现表达，像 torture、alerts、reign 等，频繁出现。

在这一部分我们学到了什么？

在给定阈值内的词语共现测量和手动检索相比更客观，尤其是检索较大的语料库时。

不同的数据检测测量词语搭配间的关联程度：共现率、t 值、交互信息值和 z 值。这些不同的测量对于分析不同类型的词是有帮助的，如 open and closed class。

词语搭配分析可以告诉我们不同的东西，比如检索项的语法环境（t 值）或者词汇环境（交互信息值、z 值）。

分析每一个文本的词汇环境和大语料库可以阐明反复出现的主题，这在一组文本或一种文化中是很重要的。

学完本章内容，我们应该可以做下列事情：

- 检索一个词或短语的常用搭配；
- 在一个具体词形和一个词目间进行选择；
- 改变词语共现的阈值；
- 通过频率检索（设定最小交互信息值）；
- 通过交互信息值检索（设定最小频率）；
- 查看检索结果，找到共现结构，例如在英式英语和美式英语中，在不同语域中（演讲、学术写作、小说等），在不同时期，等等。

更多关于词语搭配信息的话题可以在 Wendy Anderson 和 John Corbett 所著的 *Exploring English with Online Corpora* 一书中找到。

课后拓展

Searching for collocates of "terror." What frequent collocates can you find? Do any collocate surprise you?

典例示范

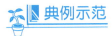

In BNC, "terror" often collocates with "reign", "sheer", "campaign", "fled" and "loyalist". In COCA, we see more words collocated with "terror." They include: "war", "attack (s)", "suspects", "acts", "against", "network", etc. There are words, like "reign" and "sheer", both used in BNC and COCA. From the results, we see that unexpectedly, some collocations have something to do with historical event.

BNC

In BNC, the three most commonly used words associated with "terror" are "reign" (54), "fear" (25), and "sheer" (22). (图 4.14)

HELP			FREQ	ALL	%	MI
1		REIGN	54	1835	2.94	7.99
2		FEAR	25	8883	0.28	4.60
3		SHEER	22	1997	1.10	6.57
4		CAMPAIGN	19	9170	0.21	4.16
5		FLED	18	1267	1.42	6.94
6		LOYALIST	13	477	2.73	7.87
7		TERROR	12	1397	0.86	6.21
8		SCREAMED	11	971	1.13	6.61
9		SCREAMING	10	1326	0.75	6.02
10		PAIN	10	6985	0.14	3.62
11		GRIPPED	9	649	1.39	6.90
12		IRA	9	1688	0.53	5.52
13		PURE	9	3384	0.27	4.52
14		SPREAD	9	6067	0.15	3.68
15		BALANCE	9	8668	0.10	3.16
16		TACTICS	8	1371	0.58	5.65
17		TUNNEL	8	2253	0.36	4.93

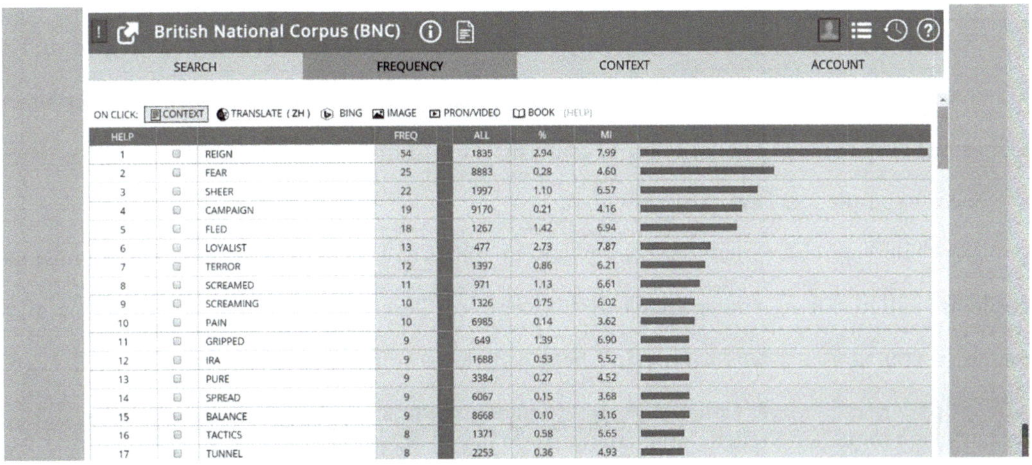

图 4.14

E.g.: a. … and her mother had imposed a reign of terror in her preparation.

b. I could see the fear and terror in your eyes when you gripped my arm and sobbed like a young child.

c. I remember the sheer terror of those raids, of seeing dead bodies lying on the pavement …

In BNC, Erebus and terror have the highest MI (11.34), followed by muggers (8.49). (图 4.15)

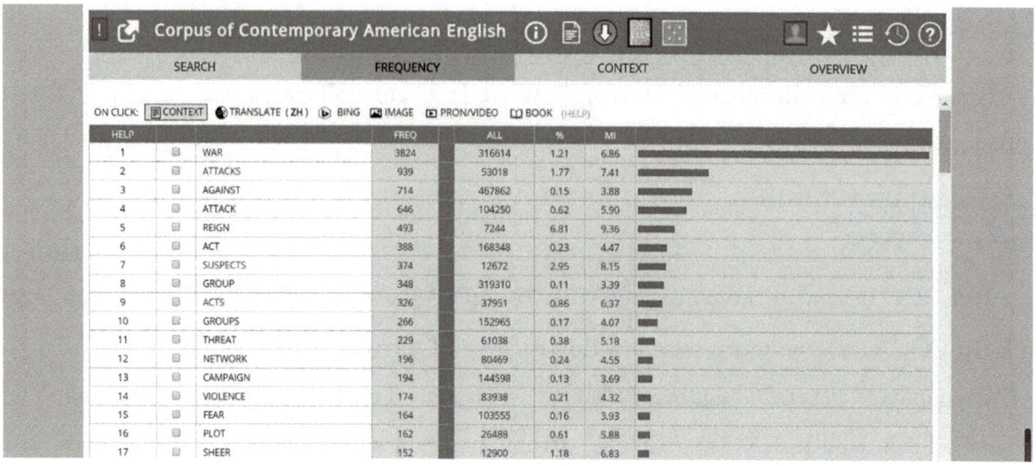

图 4.15

E. g. : one shouldn't strictly include Erebus and Terror in the same chain as those of new Zealand…

"Terror" is usually paired with words with negative meanings, such as "terror and repression." For example, women and children are bearing the brunt of continuing terror and repression used to keep the Saddam Husain dictatorships in power.

Some examples in BNC are provided.

①A/The reign of terror: normally, it can refer to the period with violence and many people are killed during that period; also, Regin of Terror is the most violent phase of the French Revolution, a year-long period between the summers of 1793 and 1794. (图 4.16)

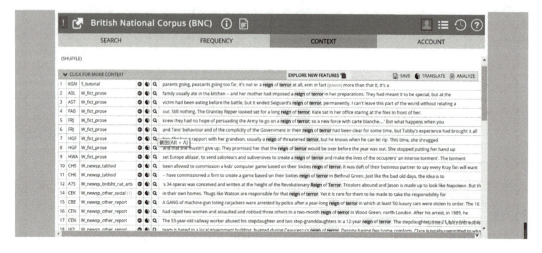

图 4.16

②Sheer terror: it can describe complete, extreme frightened. (图 4.17)

③Fled in terror: fled in terror means running away in a feeling of extreme fear. (图 4.18)

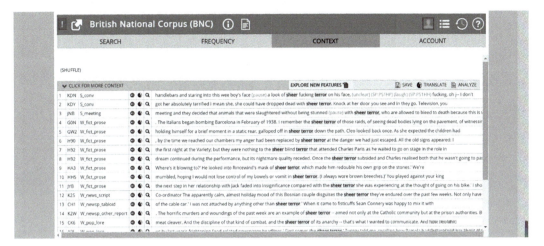

图 4.17

图 4.18

④Loyalist terror (groups/gangs): it is a particular group of people. The "Big Four" Loyalist terror groups are the Ulster Volunteer Force, the Red Hand Commando, the Ulster Defence Association and the Ulster Freedom Fighters. In 1994, the four terror groups came together under the banner of the Combined Loyalist Military Command (CLMC) to publicly unveil the loyalist ceasefire. (图 4.19)

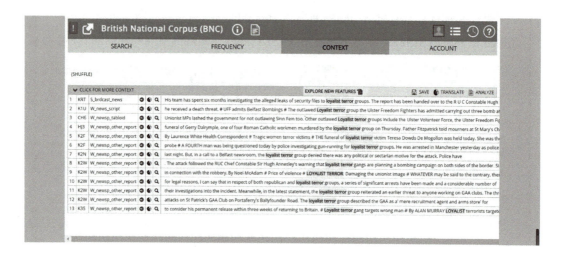

图 4.19

COCA

In COCA, the three most commonly used words coupled with "terror" are "war," (4074) "attack," (1572) and "act." (762) Words with high MI that correspond to terror include "Israel" (10.48) and "Iraq" (11.81). I think it has a lot to do with the wars that the United States has started. (图 4.20)

图 4.20

Some examples in COCA are provided.

①Acts of terror: an action is violent, or threaten violence. (图 4.21)

第四章 词语搭配

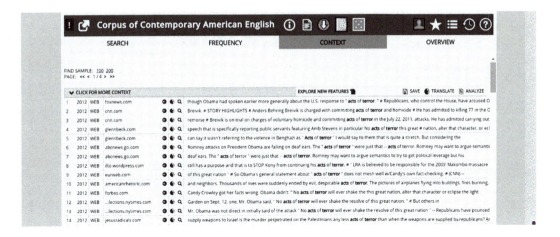

图 4.21

② Terror suspects. (图 4.22)

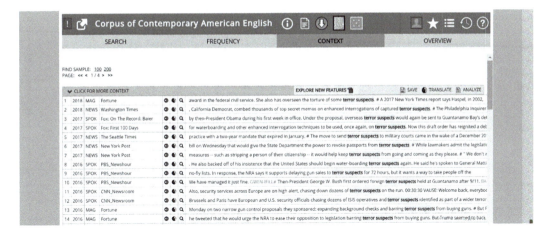

图 4.22

③ Terror attacks. (图 4.23)

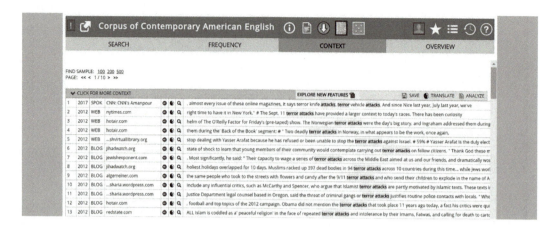

图 4.23

④War on terror: it can refer to a historical event—an international military campaign launched by the United States government after the September 11 attacks, which is also known as the Global War on Terrorism (GWOT). (图 4.24)

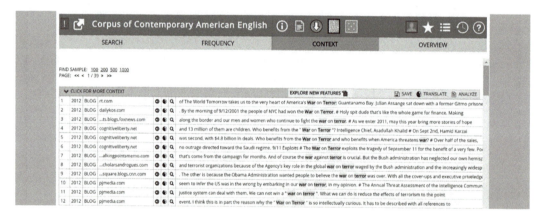

图 4.24

⑤Foil(ed) a terror plot/attack: it means preventing a plot or attack considered terrible and undesirable from succeeding, usually used in news reports.

⑥Abject terror: it's like "sheer terror," referring to a feeling of extreme fear. Both of the two phrases are useful in writing to emphasize the degree of fear. Instead of using words like "extreme," "complete", "sheer" and "abject" are more vivid and expressive.

First of all, the most frequently used word with "fear" is "reign." The collocation is "reign of fear."

E. g. : a. Her family usually ate in the kitchen, and her mother had imposed a reign of terror in her preparations.

b. As a synonym of "terror," "fear" often appears before and after "terror" to enhance the expression effect of terror.

E. g. : As it makes the bearer and the unit he is with immune to fear, terror and panic.

"Terror" is also often used with some words of degree, such as "sheer terror" means "纯粹的恐怖".

E. g. : Sheer terror in a nightmare can be the result of an unseen, hidden menace.

Collocates that are surprising.

The word "terror" was often used with some words with negative meanings. However, through the search, I found that it can also be used with some positive words.

It can collocate with "pure" to express the same meaning as "sheer terror."

E. g. : Joanna was in a state of pure terror and, although she sat down for a while, she most certainly did not sleep.

It can also collocate with "loyalist." It always appears with the form "loyalist terror groups/gangs."

E. g. : His team has spent six months investigating the alleged leaks of security files to loyalist terror groups.

第五章 类联接

语料工具

- 杨百翰大学语料库（BYU）
- 当代美国英语语料库（COCA）
- 《时代》周刊语料库（TIME）

教学内容

本章讲一讲类联接检索——colligation。从这个词的发音就能猜出 colligation 和 collocation 的区别不是很大。事实上，我们把 colligation 看作是 collocation 的变体。

词语搭配（collocation）是一个特定词或短语在距离另外一个词或短语的一定范围内所共现的词，而 colligation 指的是所共现词的词性（名词、形容词、冠词、限定词，等等），比如 fish 后面有没有动词。在本章中，我们将会讲到检索类联接的方法。

我们在杨百翰大学语料库里看看检索项的词性。我们将看到的结果是基于共现频率的，所以类联接和词语搭配是有区别的，至少中间结果是要计算的。我们没有每个共现词词性的交互信息，换句话说，我们将要学习的共现频率并不是概率。但即便是这样，我们仍可以用数据做很多事。

到目前为止，词语搭配考虑的是词和词目之间的关系：例如 coherence 的搭配词有"terror""reign""war""red""Mau Mau"，等等；neighbourhood 的搭配词（经常和语法词汇一起出现）有"the""this""my""of""on""against"，等等。

从另一方面说，类联接考虑的是词/词目与语法词的关系，例如：different＋[preposition/conjunction] or [adjective]＋[preposition]。

来看一个类联接的例子。句子"Free skiing is very different _____ traditional skiing."中缺失了什么词性的词？在横线上能够填几个词？有没有英美人士用词的方言差异？你的直觉是什么？在开始进入语料库检索之前，可以上网看看大家对于这个问题的观点。www.dailywritingtips.com 这个网站给英语学习者提供了正确使用英语的建议，其中对于使用 different 这个词的指导如下：

> "我们都对语法的用法感到抓狂,当我们听到这些东西就好像手指划过黑板的声音让人无法忍受。
> A boxer is different than a Doberman.
> This car is different to that one.
> 我觉得不只我一个人听到这样的句子会发抖,这些用法正确吗?"

可是这些用法真的不正确吗?根据 bartleby.com 的条目,different from, different to, different than,这些用法已经存在很多年了,它们都是标准的(different to 只局限于英式英语),但是,其中只有 different from 没有被质疑过。

如何在语料库中检索一个用法的频率?怎样检索美国英语和英国英语的用法?

 在线练习 1

我们可以用不同的方法检索。在杨百翰大学语料库中,可以用不同的方法找到想要的信息。要检索 different 后联用的词,我们可以在列表里找 different + preposition,或者查找后面紧跟的搭配词,然后把检索限制在介词范围内(图 5.1)。试着用任意一种方法检索吧。

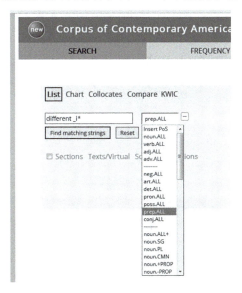

图 5.1

两种检索结果是一样的。在 COCA 中的检索结果表明 different from 出现的频率高于 different to(图 5.2)。

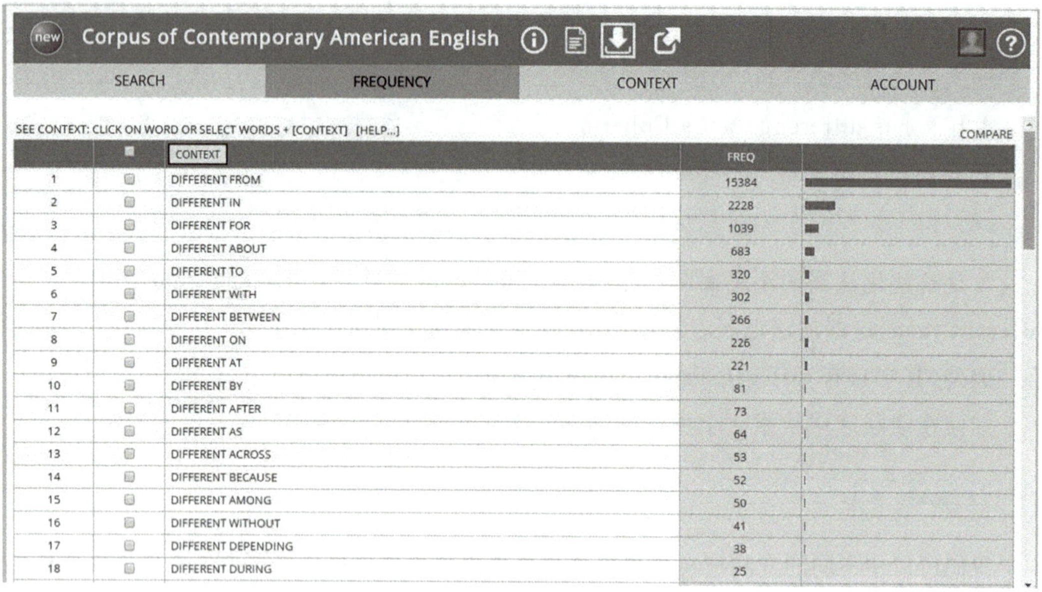

		CONTEXT	FREQ
1		DIFFERENT FROM	15384
2		DIFFERENT IN	2228
3		DIFFERENT FOR	1039
4		DIFFERENT ABOUT	683
5		DIFFERENT TO	320
6		DIFFERENT WITH	302
7		DIFFERENT BETWEEN	266
8		DIFFERENT ON	226
9		DIFFERENT AT	221
10		DIFFERENT BY	81
11		DIFFERENT AFTER	73
12		DIFFERENT AS	64
13		DIFFERENT ACROSS	53
14		DIFFERENT BECAUSE	52
15		DIFFERENT AMONG	50
16		DIFFERENT WITHOUT	41
17		DIFFERENT DEPENDING	38
18		DIFFERENT DURING	25

图 5.2

但有一个词我们没有看到，than。这是因为在 COCA 中 than 这个词不属于介词，它被归为连词。所以我们再次检索，这次查找连词而不是介词(图 5.3)。

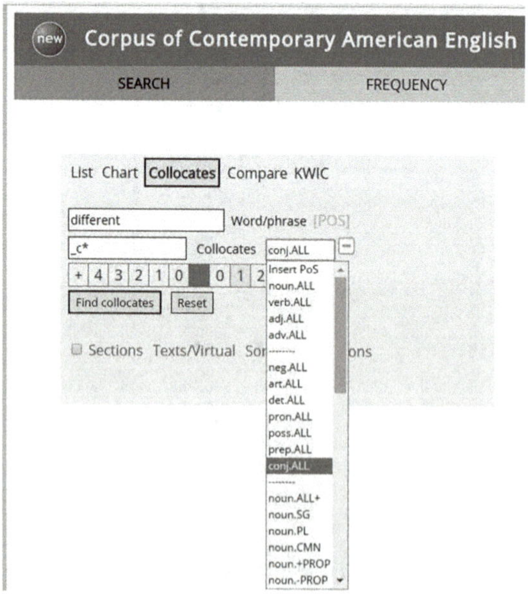

图 5.3

果然，than 是紧跟在 different 之后出现的频率最高的连词(图 5.4)。如果我们比较介词出现的频率，则 COCA 中的结果显示 from 和 in 是按照频率顺序跟在 different 之后的(图 5.5)。

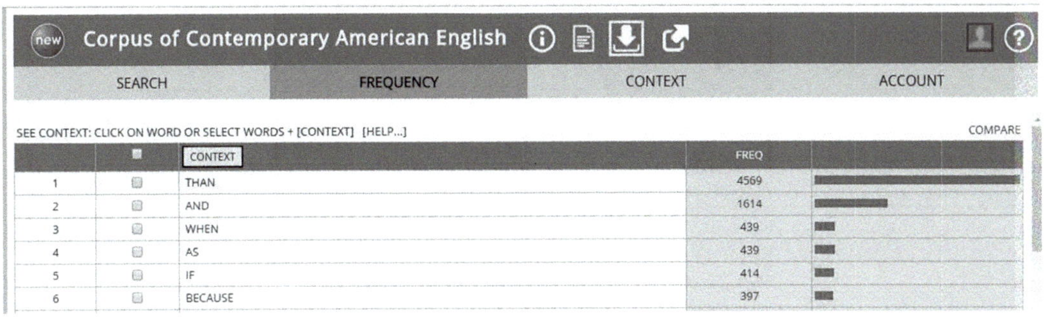

		CONTEXT	FREQ
1		THAN	4569
2		AND	1614
3		WHEN	439
4		AS	439
5		IF	414
6		BECAUSE	397

图 5.4

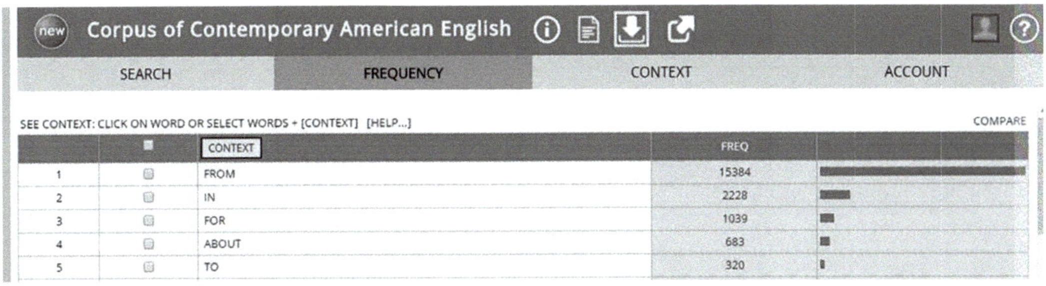

		CONTEXT	FREQ
1		FROM	15384
2		IN	2228
3		FOR	1039
4		ABOUT	683
5		TO	320

图 5.5

现在来比较 COCA 和 BNC 的结果(记得把频率设为标准值)。因为在 COCA 中有 5 亿 2 000 万个词,而在 BNC 只有 1 亿个词,所以必须将 BNC 检索结果的值乘以 5.2,这样才可以进行比较。看看 BNC 的检索结果(图 5.6—图 5.7),你会发现 different than 在 BNC 中出现频率很低(图 5.6),即使我们把结果(50)乘以 5.2(=260),还是比 COCA 中的出现频率 4569(图 5.4)低很多。因此我们可以肯定地说美国人倾向于使用 different than。

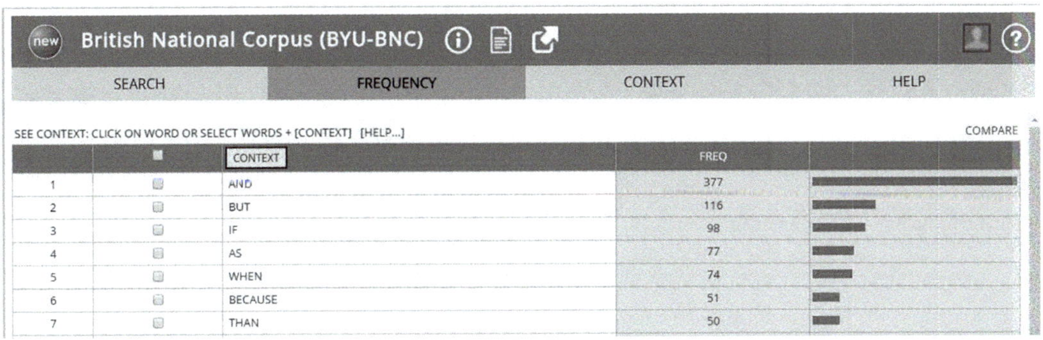

		CONTEXT	FREQ
1		AND	377
2		BUT	116
3		IF	98
4		AS	77
5		WHEN	74
6		BECAUSE	51
7		THAN	50

图 5.6

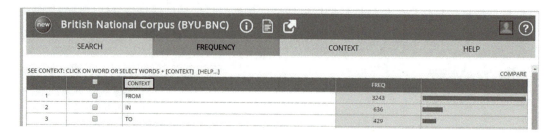

图 5.7

在线练习 2

假设 different than 在美国英语中很普遍,现在我们来做一个历时的检索,可以借助 TIME 进行。(图 5.8)

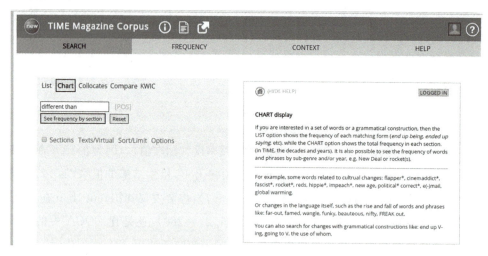

图 5.8

可以看到,20 世纪 90 年代开始,different than 出现的频率激增(图 5.9)。再来看看近二十余年的例子(图 5.10),可以发现 different than 在两种不同的语境中使用。你能认出它们吗?

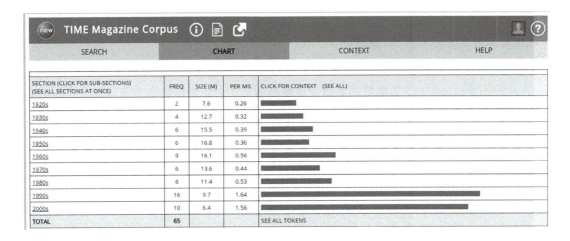

图 5.9

图 5.10

从不同的检索中,我们可以得出以下结论:

①different from 仍是英美人士倾向的用法。

②different to 可能是英式英语的变体。(在美国不常见,尽管有这种嵌入结构,像 X means [something different] to Y。)

③different than 在英式英语中不太常见,但这种用法日渐增多。TIME 语料库表明这种用法在增加,经常用于引出从句:X is no different than it was Y。

下面进一步探索 than 的位置的改变。很可能是因为它的语法功能主要是从属连词,所以引出从句跟在 different 之后。但是这个词越来越多地被当作介词使用,如"X is different than Y",它的语法功能是在 20 世纪 90 年代转变的。

本章介绍了如何通过语料库来解决类联接,更多的例子可以参考 Dee Gardner 和 Mark Davies 在 2007 年发表的文章 *Pointing Out Frequent Phrasal Verbs*:*A Corpus Based Analysis*,*TESOL Quarterly*(Vol. 41,No. 2,June,pp. 339-359),这篇文章提到一系列跟语言教师相关的关于类联接的问题:

哪些动词短语(或多词动词)在英语中最普遍?

哪些是最有效产的实义动词？

哪些是最有效的小品词（虚词）？

哪些是最常见的联合？

Gardner 和 Davies 的文章是怎么回答这些问题的？

Which phrasal verbs (or multi-word verbs) are the most common in English?

Which are the most productive lexical verbs?

Which are the most productive particles?

Which are the commonest combinations?

How does the article Gardner and Davies (2007) answer them?

典例示范

1. Which phrasal verbs (or multi-word verbs) are the most common in English?

"Go around," "come around," "turn around," "bring about" and "come along" are the most common phrasal verbs in English.

Table 5.1 suggests that "go," (227 103) "get," (213 726) and "make" (210 880) are the most common verbs in English. There are six verbs ranked in the top 10 (GO, 2; GET, 3; MAKE, 4; TAKE, 7; COME, 9; GIVE, 10), and four others in the top 20 (LOOK, 11; FIND, 13; PUT, 16; WORK, 19). These prolific verbs' function 24.2% of the time in PV constructions underscores the importance of English PVs.

The combination of Table 5.1 and Table 5.2 suggests that "go around," "come around," "turn around," "bring about," and "come along" are the most common phrasal verbs in English.

Table 5.1 Descriptive Statistics of Top 20 Lexical Verb (LV) Lemmas Functioning in Phrasal Verb (PV) Forms

LV lemma	# in BNC PVs	% of all BNC PVs	Cum% of all BNC PVs	Total # in BNC	BNC rank	% as PVs
GO	48 016	9.3	9.3	227 103	2	21.1
COME	36 878	7.1	16.4	145 047	9	25.4
TAKE	22 970	4.4	20.8	173 996	7	13.2
GET	20 223	3.9	24.7	213 726	3	9.5
SET	18 569	3.6	28.3	39 149	40	47.4

Cont.

LV lemma	# in BNC PVs	% of all BNC PVs	Cum% of all BNC PVs	Total # in BNC	BNC rank	% as PVs
CARRY	15 617	3.0	31.3	30 572	53	51.1
TURN	13 040	2.5	33.8	44 051	32	29.6
BRING	12 514	2.4	36.2	42 567	33	29.4
LOOK	12 226	2.4	38.6	109 110	11	11.2
PUT	11 970	2.3	40.9	67 839	16	17.6
PICK	9 997	1.9	42.8	14 274	138	70.0
MAKE	7 368	1.4	44.2	210 880	4	3.5
POINT	7 159	1.4	45.6	13 767	149	52.0
SIT	7 112	1.4	47.0	27 388	64	26.0
FIND	6 934	1.3	48.3	96 010	13	7.2
GIVE	6 174	1.2	49.5	125 312	10	4.9
WORK	5 985	1.2	50.6	63 104	19	9.5
BREAK	5 428	1.0	51.7	18 642	109	29.1
HOLD	5 403	1.0	52.7	46 773	30	11.6
MOVE	5 197	1.0	53.7	37 820	41	13.7
Total	278 780	53.7	53.7	1 747 130	39*	24.2*

Note: # = token frequency. Cum% = cumulative frequency percentage. Values based on nonseparable and separable counts (i.e., verb [V] + adverbial phrase [AVP], V + X + AVP, V + X X + AVP). Total phrasal verb (PV) tokens in the British National Corpus (BNC) = 518 923; total lexical verb (LV) tokens in BNC = 10 404 107. * = Average of column.

Table 5.2 Verb Particle Frequencies of Top 20 Lexical Verbs Functioning in Phrasal Verb (PV) Forms

Round	About	Through	Around	Along	Under	By	Across	Total
1 366	244	972	394	717	95	44	0	48 016
1 107	741	567	139	1 270	2	7	0	36 878
78	2	31	37	94	0	0	0	22 970

Cont.

Round	About	Through	Around	Along	Under	By	Across	Total
365	102	533	241	163	3	42	1	20 223
0	645	0	0	0	0	0	0	18 569
10	29	127	107	52	0	0	0	15 617
1 146	38	1	423	0	4	0	0	13 040
105	2 083	11	18	88	0	0	0	12 514
694	45	21	779	0	0	0	0	12 226
21	35	90	16	1	9	0	5	11 970
0	0	0	0	0	0	0	0	9 997
16	0	40	2	8	0	0	0	7 368
0	0	0	0	0	0	0	0	7 159
34	18	4	126	1	1	0	0	7 112
3	3	10	29	0	0	0	0	6 934
3	1	0	2	0	0	0	0	6 174
23	0	100	19	5	10	0	0	5 985
0	0	169	0	0	0	0	0	5 428
2	0	0	1	0	4	0	0	5 403
19	178	2	340	84	0	0	0	5 197
4 992	4 164	2 678	2 673	2 483	128	93	6	278 780
1.0	0.8	0.5	0.5	0.5	0.0	0.0	0.0	53.7
51.4	52.2	52.7	53.2	53.7	53.7	53.7	53.7	

Note: Cum % = cumulative frequency percentage.

2. Which are the most productive lexical verbs?

Table 5.3 suggests that "carry out" (10 798) and "set up" (10 360) are the most common in English.

We can see that only 25 PV lemmas make up nearly one third (30.4%) of all PV occurrences in BNC. Fifty PV lemmas constitute 42.7% of the total, and only 100 are needed to cover more than one half (51.4%) of all PV occurrences in BNC.

Table 5.3 Verb-Particle Frequencies of Top 20 Lexical Verbs Functioning in Phrasal Verb (PV) Forms

Verb	Out	Up	On	Back	Down	In	Off	Over
GO	7 688	3 678	14 903	8 065	4 781	1 974	2 104	991
COME	5 022	5 523	4 830	8 029	3 305	4 814	518	1 004
TAKE	3 426	4 608	4 199	1 628	775	509	2 163	5 420
GET	3 545	3 936	2 696	4 552	1 538	1 127	1 086	293
SET	4 633	10 360	11	265	504	281	1 869	1
CARRY	10 798	36	3 869	172	84	32	170	131
TURN	4 284	2 710	292	1 378	1 051	149	594	975
BRING	1 425	2 507	390	2 200	1 022	2 505	31	129
LOOK	1 641	3 871	244	2 251	2 221	250	2	207
PUT	1 660	2 835	1 428	1 369	2 873	810	742	76
PICK	856	9 037	35	3	3	1	44	18
MAKE	1 105	5 469	25	270	65	16	277	75
POINT	6 984	104	0	7	56	0	6	2
SIT	191	1 158	118	834	4 478	145	1	3
FIND	6 619	33	9	128	34	57	4	5
GIVE	532	4 186	34	507	11	579	121	198
WORK	4 703	334	411	36	98	182	33	31
BREAK	996	1 286	3	4	2 199	220	549	2
HOLD	1 507	1 624	908	823	369	34	91	40
MOVE	573	477	1 419	566	306	790	242	201
Total	68 188	63 772	35 824	33 082	25 773	14 475	10 647	9 802
% of PV	13.1	12.3	6.9	6.4	5.0	2.8	2.1	1.9
Cum %	13.1	25.4	32.3	38.7	43.7	46.5	48.5	50.4

3. Which are the most productive particles?

There are eight most prolific particles: out, up, on, back, down, in, off and over. They combine with the 20 lexical verb lemmas to account for approximately one-half of all phrasal verb tokens in BNC.

It is also clear from the values in Table 5.4 that certain forms are more likely to act as particles than as prepositions. In particular, out (97.3%), up (87.4%), down (79.2%), and back (77.4%) occur much more often as AVPs in PV constructions than they do as prepositions in prepositional phrases.

Table 5.4 Frequency of Adverbial Particles (AVPs) in BNC

Form	Total tags	# as AVP	% as AVP
out	149 727	145 706	97.3
up	180 792	158 064	87.4
down	91 832	72 709	79.2
back	97 154	75 233	77.4
of	67 479	37 751	55.9
round	30 821	10 895	35.3
along	18 555	4 925	26.5
over	128 304	32 526	25.4
around	43 391	10 384	23.9
on	705 790	54 956	7.8
through	81 184	5 797	7.1
about	190 615	12 587	6.6
in	1 845 077	34 411	1.9
under	60 049	313	0.5
by	504 969	371	0.1
across	24 053	13	0.1
Total	4 219 792	656 641	15.6

4. Which are the commonest combinations?

Table 5.5 displays the word-sense frequencies from WordNet for the top 100 PVs in BNC, which can reveal the commonest combination. From this graph, we can conclude that "break up," "pick up," "take in," "set up," "take out" are the commonest combinations.

Table 5.5 Number of WordNet Senses for Top 100 Phrasal Verbs (PVs) in BNC

PV	Senses	PV	Senses	PV	Senses	PV	Senses
go on	5	carry on	4	put on	9	move in	3
carry out	2	go up	7	bring out	9	look around	1
set up	15	get out	7	move on	1	take down	4
pick up	16	take out	14	turn back	2	put off	5
go back	4	come down	5	put back	2	come about	1
come back	5	put down	7	go round * *	5	go along	3
go out	6	put up	8	break up	19	look round * * *	0
point out	3	turn up	5	come along	2	set about	3
find out	4	get on	7	sit up	2	turn off	3
come up	12	bring up	8	turn round * *	3	give in	2
make up	8	bring in	5	get in	5	move out	10
take over	8	look back	2	come round * *	1	come through	4
comne out	11	look down *	5	make out	10	move back	5
come on	5	bring back	2	get off	11	break off	5
come in	5	break down	8	turn down	5	get through	5
go down	8	take off	9	bring down	6	give out	4
work out	8	go off	6	come over	1	come off	3
set out	3	bring about	5	break out	5	take in	17
take up	13	go in	1	go over	9	give back	1
get back	4	set off	7	turn over	9	set down	6
sit down	3	put out	10	go through	5	move up	2
turn out	12	look out	2	hold on	5	turn around+	0
take on	5	take back	6	pick ou	2		
give up	12	hold up	7	sit back	2		
get up	8	get down	7	hold back	5		
look up	1	hold out	5	put in	7		

Note: Total senses = 559. PV = phrasal verb. * Consulted *Longman Dictionary of Phrasal Verbs* (Courtney, 1993). * * WordNet = *around*. * * * See *look around*. +See *turn round*.

第六章　关键词索引分布

语料工具

● AntConc 文本分析工具

教学内容

观察关键词检索行时，我们考虑一个词或短语是如何在其前后 4~5 个词的语境中构成的；检索词语搭配时，我们考虑在一个文本中频率和词汇共现的可能性；关注类联接时，我们检索和检索项共同出现的语法结构；而有时候了解在一段文本中，一个词或一组相关词汇出现在什么地方是很有用的。有些文本分析工具，像免费软件 AntConc 或付费软件 wordsmith，都可以向用户展示关键词索引分布（也就是词汇在文本中出现的位置）：这个词是频繁地出现在文本的开头、中间还是结尾，抑或是有规律地出现在整个文本中？

本章利用 AntConc 文本分析工具进行关键词索引分布检索。这个检索工具是由日本早稻田大学的劳伦斯·安东尼（Laurence Anthony）设计开发的。

首先，需要下载 AntConc 软件，可以在早稻田大学官网作者的个人页面上下载。

其次，需要一个文本或一些文本来进行分析。可以在网上选择，比如 Project Gutenberg 网站中的没有版权的文章，或者是新闻报道。文本量可以大，也可以小。举个例子，选择一篇 BBC 的新闻报道，这是一篇苏格兰民族党领袖亚历克斯·萨尔蒙德（Alex Salmond）的演讲。我们对它做一些改动，把照片和额外的信息删掉，只包含所要分析文章的文本，然后以文本文件的形式保存。

打开 AntConc 软件，使用 Open File 加载文本，点击 File View 并检查一下文本，如果没有问题，就可以点击 Word List 生成特定词汇的频率，也可以点击关键词索引生成关键词索引行（例如检索 independence 这个单词）。

如果想知道这篇文本中 independence 这个词出现在哪，可以点击 Concordance Plot，文本下方立刻就会出现一连串的词。有意思的是，如果不看整篇文本，只选择抽样演讲稿的开头或结尾部分，那么在 independence 的上方或下方会出现这个词的出现频率。

需要强调的是，知道在一篇或更多文本中特定的单词或短语在什么位置是很有用的。你可以自己选择文本，用一系列词条或语法条目试试。你预计哪类词在文本里更有规律地出现？可以在任意一篇文本中检测一下你的假设。

一些文本分析工具,像 AntConc,让我们看到词汇的构成或分布。我们可以直观地看到词汇在哪成团出现。再比较文本,我们会看到特定表达的相似性或不同。

至此我们已经了解了几种不同的检索工具。每一种分析文本的方式都不同,尽管它们相互关联。需要关注的工具有频率、人工解释关键词索引、数据测量词语搭配(交互信息值、t 值、z 值)、类联接、关键词索引分布等。

如何用这些工具探究问题?

1. 探究词汇变化和创新:一些词,像 globalisation、teenage、adolescent、same-sex、mentor、downsize 等,是如何进入到语言中的?其他词,比如 scullery,这个词已经消失了吗?还有多次出现但意义完全不同的词 wireless。

2. 探究语形变化和创新:后缀,像-nik、-gate、-ista,是如何进入和分散在语言中的?而那些特定词汇,如 flammable、inflammable、uninflammable 呢?

TIME 语料库的频率检索(以每十年一个图表分类)告诉我们 scullery(一个老式词汇)意为厨房,后来在 20 世纪逐渐衰退(至少在美国期刊中)。(这可以被看作是这个词几十年间在美式英语和英式英语中流行程度的索引。)

TIME 语料库的频率检索也可以表明 wireless 的不同结构:在 20 世纪早期这个词开始流行,作为无线电接收话语的一部分;随着无线电技术的变化,这个词开始衰落,取而代之的一些表达变得流行起来;在互联网时代,wireless 又回来了,但是概念与之前完全不同。

我们还可以问一些关于句法而不是语法的问题。

3. 英式英语或美式英语中使用频率最高的动词短语是什么?get-passive 在英语中如何使用?end-up 加动词-ing 在英语中如何使用?

也可以问一些语义方面的问题。

4. 词汇的本意和典型意思是一回事还是有所不同?gather 的"收集"这个意义用得最频繁还是"明白、理解"这个意义用得最频繁?gay、lame、green 这些词的意义和 20 年前比有什么变化?

此外,也可以提出一些关于话语的问题。

5. 在性别、环境、政治、恐怖主义、革命或移民等文本中,某个单词,跟 10 年、30 年、100 年前比有什么不同?

6. 在关于性别、环境、政治、恐怖主义的文本中,一些特定的词或短语,比如 woman、battle 或 I,是如何分布的?

现在提出一个你感兴趣的问题。你会如何开始探究?你会优先选择哪一种语料库检索工具?

第七章 主题词分析

📝 语料工具

- 杨百翰大学语料(BYU)
- 英国国家语料库(BNC)

👤 教学内容

本章中学习最后一种检索方式：主题词分析。主题词在语料库语言学中是一个模糊的概念。你可能还记得关键词索引检索，有时也被称为上下文关键词检索。关键词节点就是指主题词。而在本章中，主题词所指则有所不同。

到目前为止，我们了解了在语料库中检索词频，尝试了人工解释关键词索引行，也见到了词语搭配和类关联的数据分析，还使用 AntConc 软件来检索关键词索引分布。我们已经做了很多，但是我们一直在关注个体语料库的分析，或者是 COCA，或者是 BNC，或者是 TIME。如果想把一个词在某个语料库出现的频率和它在另外一个语料库中的频率对比，该怎么办呢？例如，一些特定表达是不是在美语语料库或英式英语语料库出现得更频繁或很不频繁？要回答这个问题，我们可以对比语料库，分析主题词。

什么是主题词分析？主题词分析就是通过比较两个语料库，发现在所研究的语料库中异常频繁或异常罕见的词语。换句话说，我们要比较两个语料库，一个是专用语料库，一个是参照语料库。为什么我们会对异常频繁或异常罕见的词感兴趣？通常这些（主题）词是专用语料库中有文化倾向性的东西。如果我们将一个商务报道语料库和一个通用语料库作比较，找出在专业语料库中出现得异常频繁的词，我们可以猜测，它们一定是些与特定商务报道语料和文化有关的东西。并且，那些在专用语料库中非常频繁出现的词在通用语料库中出现时也可以间接告诉我们一些与特定领域有关的东西。主题词分析要使用公式，例如，用对数似然比来计算那些跟另外一个语料库相比频率高或低的词。本章使用 AntConc 软件来确定短语在语料库中的主题性。

用 AntConc 软件或其他检索软件（如 Wordsmith）进行主题词分析时，需要有一些基本数据。首先需要一个专用语料库 A 和一个参照语料库 B。通常参照语料库比专用语料库更大、更通用，但是并不总是如此。这取决于你想让主题词分析做什么。

专用语料库和参照语料库的特性将由研究的问题决定（还有一些其他方面的考虑，

如可及性)。

比较新闻专用语料库 A 和通用语料库 BNC 或 COCA,可以发现语料库 A 中有意义的词;将新闻专用语料库 A 和同体裁参照语料库 B 进行对比,可以发现与语料库 B 相对的语料库 A 中的有意义的词。当然,也可以只比较同一语料库的部分内容,例如,拿 COCA 和 BNC 中的口语部分作为专用语料库,然后跟同一个语料库中的书面语部分进行比较。

 在线练习

下面来操作试试。我们在网上找到一篇演讲稿(图 7.1),建一个专用语料库(保存为文本文件,见图 7.2。也可以添加更多此类型的文本。

图 7.1

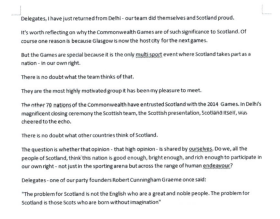

图 7.2

下一步有点复杂,我们需要确定和演讲内容进行对比的东西。这篇演讲稿可以和一系列其他类型的语料库,如通用写作语料库、通用口语语料库、影视剧语料库,或者其他任何语料库进行对比。参照语料库的选择很重要,改变了参照物,描述就会改变。我们选择苏格兰英语语料库。访问苏格兰英语语料库网页,点击高级搜索,再从菜单栏中选择 written record of speech(演讲书面记录)。

然后,我们在苏格兰英语语料库中选择苏格兰议会主体文本,点击下载并保存为压缩文件。将下载的内容解压缩(图 7.3)并保存为纯文本文件,文件名为"议会参照语料库"。我们将找到的演讲稿和苏格兰英语语料库中其他普通的政治性演讲进行比较。

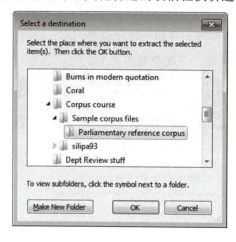

图 7.3

我们现在有了专用语料库和参照语料库,就可以使用 AntConc 软件进行文本分析了。打开 AntConc 软件,点击 File,选择 Open,将我们保存的演讲稿文件上传到专用语料库中,如图 7.4 和图 7.5 所示。

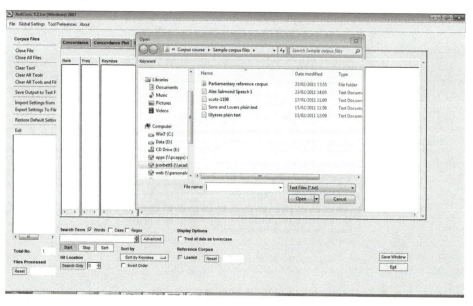

图 7.4

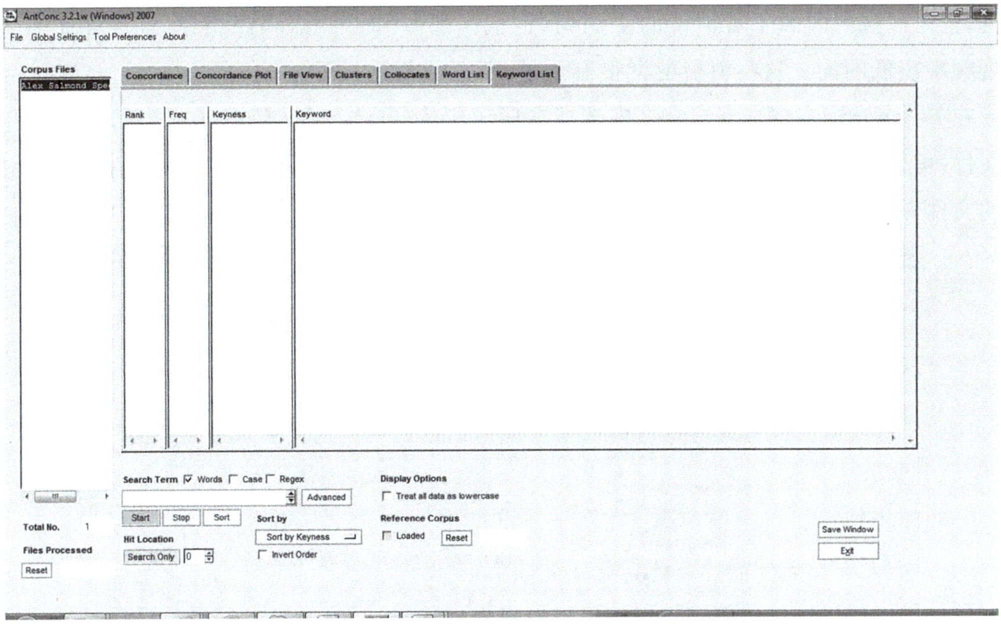

图 7.5

点击 Tool Preferences，选择 Keyword List，如图 7.6 所示。

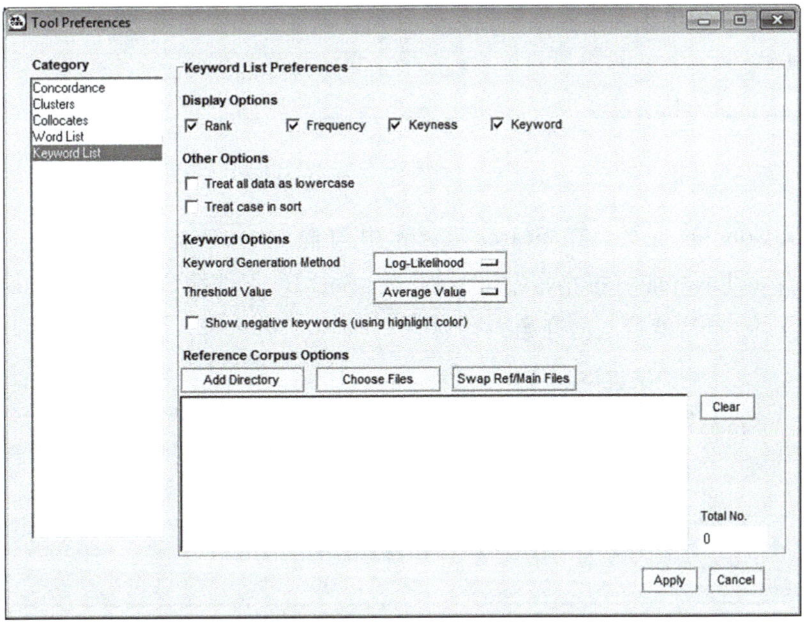

图 7.6

选择 Keyword Options（主题性）统计量度。像词语搭配一样，有很多种方法可以计算这个统计量度，用得最多的就是对数似然比，方差是另外一种选择。这里选择 Log-Likehood

（对数似然比）。我们可以为要展示的主题词的数量设置一个门槛，如我们想看前100个主题词，也可以选择看或不看消极的主题词（也就是那些和参照语料库相比，在专用语料库中出现频率超低的词。这些消极的词很有意思，所以我们选择看）。

在 Keyword List Preferences 中选择参照语料库（Reference Corpus）。（如果我们有多个文件，可以选择 directory，即含有这些文件的文件夹。）我们选择刚才下载的存有参照语料库的文件夹，如图7.7所示，然后点击 Apply。

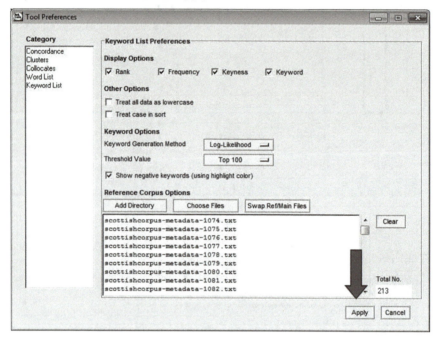

图7.7

回到 AntConc 的主页。在 Search Term 中勾选 Words，在 Display Options 中勾选 Treat all data as lowercase（按小写字母处理），在 Sort by 下选择 Sort by Keyness（按主题性排序），如图7.8所示，然后点击开始。

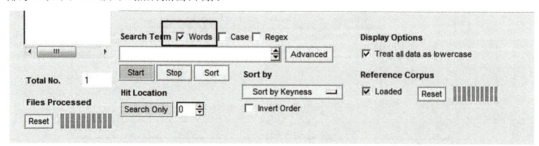

图7.8

如果幸运的话，我们会得到一组结果（图7.9）。花些时间来看看这些词。我们如何解读这些结果？

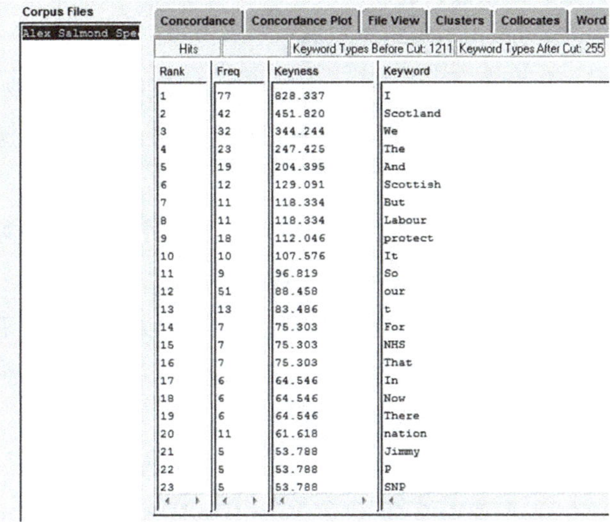
Corpus Files | Alex Salmond Spe
Concordance | Concordance Plot | File View | Clusters | Collocates | Word
Hits | Keyword Types Before Cut: 1211 | Keyword Types After Cut: 255

Rank	Freq	Keyness	Keyword
1	77	828.337	I
2	42	451.820	Scotland
3	32	344.244	We
4	23	247.425	The
5	19	204.395	And
6	12	129.091	Scottish
7	11	118.334	But
8	11	118.334	Labour
9	18	112.046	protect
10	10	107.576	It
11	9	96.819	So
12	51	88.458	our
13	13	83.486	t
14	7	75.303	For
15	7	75.303	NHS
16	7	75.303	That
17	6	64.546	In
18	6	64.546	Now
19	6	64.546	There
20	11	61.618	nation
21	5	53.788	Jimmy
22	5	53.788	P
23	5	53.788	SNP

(a)

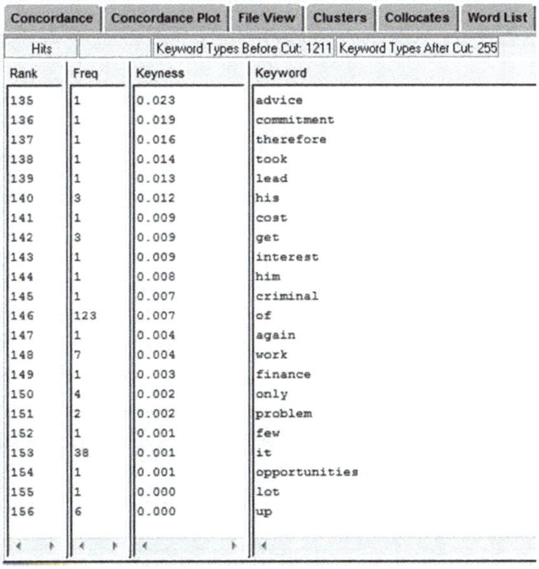
Concordance | Concordance Plot | File View | Clusters | Collocates | Word List
Hits | Keyword Types Before Cut: 1211 | Keyword Types After Cut: 255

Rank	Freq	Keyness	Keyword
135	1	0.023	advice
136	1	0.019	commitment
137	1	0.016	therefore
138	1	0.014	took
139	1	0.013	lead
140	3	0.012	his
141	1	0.009	cost
142	3	0.009	get
143	1	0.009	interest
144	1	0.008	him
145	1	0.007	criminal
146	123	0.007	of
147	1	0.004	again
148	7	0.004	work
149	1	0.003	finance
150	4	0.002	only
151	2	0.002	problem
152	1	0.001	few
153	38	0.001	it
154	1	0.001	opportunities
155	1	0.000	lot
156	6	0.000	up

(b)

图 7.9

我们注意到一些不寻常的词。

①I/we:是仅指演讲者自身,还是将听众也包含在内?(注意 I 用在句子结尾处的加强。)

②Scotland/Scottish/nation:这篇演讲是有关民族主义的吗?

③Labor:(在苏格兰)是演讲者(Alex Salmond)所在政党主要的政治对手。

④protect/NHS：政府作为照料者。

⑤人名(Jimmy＝ally；Cameron＝enemy)。

我们注意到这篇演讲中 finance/cost 出现的频率比较低，还有(和普通政治性演讲相比) problem 出现频率也不高。这篇演讲似乎在刻意避免经济或麻烦。(这是一个让人沮丧的演讲吗?)

总之，发现是有启发性的。但是单独使用主题词分析时要谨慎，最好是将这种分析和其他的分析结合起来。

下面我们在这篇演讲里识别主题词。可以使用关键词索引分布看看它们出现在文本中的什么地方。加载专用语料库并选择关键词索引分布，然后检索感兴趣的主题词。game 这个单词在文本中出现了 4 次，而 I 出现了 77 次。

关键词索引分布表明 game 在演讲的开头部分出现 4 次(图 7.10)。

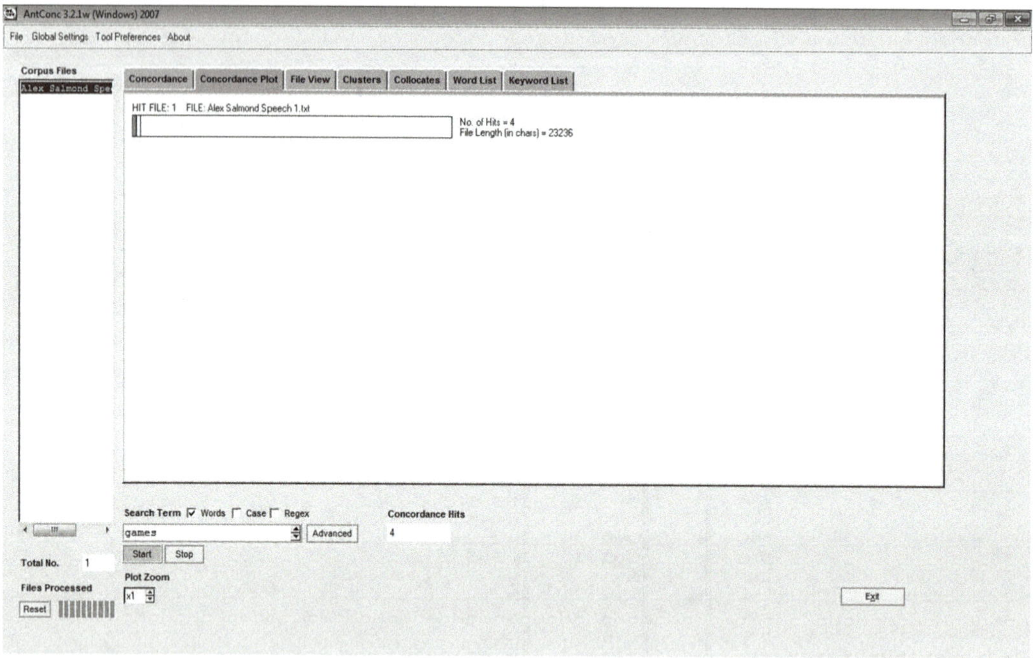

图 7.10

而代词 I 分布在整个演讲中(图 7.11)，甚至被用在结束部分来加强语气。(也许有一种强烈的个人责任感或力量在演讲中被表达出来，我们可以再回头看看演讲内容进一步确认。)和其他政治演讲文本相比，I 在这篇演讲中出现得异常频繁，并且在结尾处尤甚。我们可以想想，这有什么隐含意义吗?

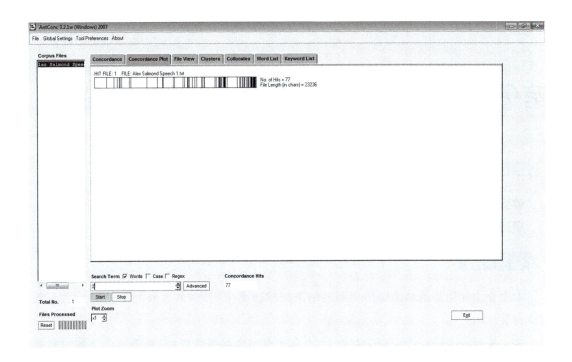

图 7.11

现在来总结一下,当我们比较语料库时,就会用到主题词分析。而统计公式,像对数似然比或者方差,被用来计算在那些相对于另一个语料库而言,在该语料库中异常频繁出现或异常罕见的词。这类分析可以告诉我们很多有趣的跟内容有关的东西,如文本风格和意识形态。我们可以把主题词分析和其他类型的分析(比如关键词索引分布)相结合,来增强我们对文本作用的理解。

第八章　语料库语言学的应用：词典编纂

语料工具

- 杨百翰大学语料库(BYU)
- 当代美国英语语料库(COCA)

教学内容

本章介绍如何将语料库应用到不同的语言学研究中，其中最重要的驱动应用之一就是词典编纂。

首先来看一看语料库语言学在过去40年中对词典编纂的影响，看看词典编纂学家是如何利用如关键词索引检索这些语料库工具的。我们还要看看在语料库时代，词典的定义。

在具体介绍之前，我们先来想想，在语料库出现之前，编纂词典是如何开展的。图8.1所示是早期牛津英语词典编纂工作的现场。在那时的缮写室里，我们可以看到牛津英语词典曾经的编纂者，詹姆斯·穆雷(James Murray)和他的助手。那时的编写条件非常艰苦，天气很冷，他们把脚放在装满稻草的盒子里取暖。他们把志愿者们读完的书一页页筛查，记录下有趣的词。穆雷和他的助手把这些信息进行编辑和补充，并把它们放进词典里。这个工作花费数十年才完成。从1879年起穆雷受雇编写词典，到1928年，穆雷去世后13年，第一版牛津词典才正式出版。

图8.1

牛津英文词典是建立在人工阅读的基础上的,按词源进行编纂。牛津英语词典的词条包含很多信息:要界定的词,其词性,读音、拼写,词源和本义,对其每一个意义的界定和例证(证明这个意义并说明其用法)。

牛津英语词典是一个了不起的成就,早在电脑时代到来前就完成了。然而,它是不是能给出任何我们想从字典中得到的东西?不同的读者想要什么?读者真的想知道某个词的词源吗?也许他们只想知道这个词在今天是怎么用的;如果这个词经常用在口语和写作中,就值得把它记住;或者能够同这个词搭配的词和短语。这些东西,语料库可以很容易地告诉我们,而且与人工阅读相比要精确很多。

一本词典改变了一切。*Collins Cobuild*(柯林斯词典)出版于 1987 年,这本词典使用的语料库在现在看来很小,只有 2000 万个词,但足以影响词典编纂时的选词及意义。

Susan Hunston 在她的书 *Corpora in Applied Linguistics* 中指出,语料库让今天的词典编纂者做到 20 世纪早期所不能做的事,即使是那些在 Murray 的缮写室里的英雄们。具体来说,词典编纂者可以:

①给出每一个词不同意思的更多信息;

②给出每个词和短语出现频率的精确信息;

③提供更多具体的关于词语搭配和用词的信息;

④宣告对每个意义的原始引用,尤其是这些意义是从语料库数据中获得的(尽管对于使用语料库数据来解释词汇意义还有争议)。

我们来看看要界定的词的各层含义。有一个常见的英语词 know,如果你去图书馆找一本在柯林斯词典出版之前的词典,你会发现有相当数量的词义未被列出。比如,1987 年版的朗文词典,为动词 know 列出了 20 种独立的含义;1995 年的柯林斯词典第 2 版列出了 30 多种含义;1995 年出版的以语料库为依据编纂的朗文词典列出了超过 40 种含义。现在的柯林斯词典列出了它的 39 种主要意思外加一系列跟 know 连用的短语。语料库将焦点聚集在很多普通词汇的意义上,使用户可以了解到很多词语的细微差别。在我们继续学习之前,想想这对于纸质词典页码的影响。

有一个降低纸质词典成本的办法是上网。MACMILLAN 在线词典就是以语料库为依据编纂的。它使用色标编码并界定了那些在语言中频繁使用的词,尤其适合英语学习者。语料库语言学让我们知道了 90% 的英语语句中只使用了 7500 个词,而词典里大量的其他词只被剩下 10% 的英语语句所使用。所以,如果你学会了 7500 个核心词汇,你就可以理解 90% 的英语语句。MACMILLAN 英语词典用红色将这 7500 个词编码,并用一颗星、两颗星、三颗星将出现最频繁的词标出,如 hope(图 8.2)。这些标星的词都是值得记住的词。如果你是一个教材编写者,这些词汇大概率会出现在教学资料里。

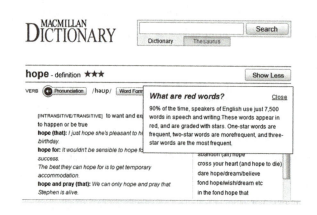

图 8.2

我们再来看一个出现频率不高的词——kow-tow(kowtow),这是一个源于汉语的外来语词汇,其首要意义来自书面英语的例证,最早出现在旅行者的游记里。这个词在 MACMILLAN 词典里(图 8.3)可能不会引起人们的兴趣,但在牛津英文词典里就不一样了(图 8.4)。

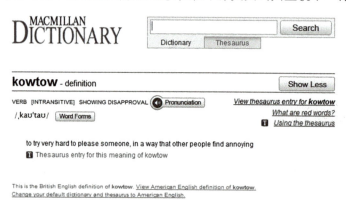

图 8.3

图 8.4

第八章 语料库语言学的应用：词典编纂

在线练习

词典编纂者还可以将频率信息用在其他方面。在英语里，record 这个词可以是名词也可以是动词，那么哪种形式在词典里首先出现？如果想把使用最多的形式放在第一位，可以在语料库中进行检索，将名词形式和动词形式出现的频率相比较，看看孰高孰低。我们可以很容易地用在线语料库（如 COCA）进行列表检索，如图 8.5 所示。（在方括号里输入词性，中间没有空格。）

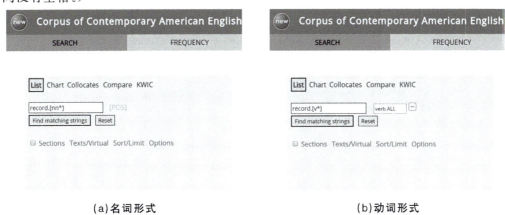

(a)名词形式　　　　　　　　　　(b)动词形式

图 8.5

在 2017 年初，record 这个词在 COCA 里标记为作为名词出现的频率比作为动词高近 8 倍（作为名词出现了 65 686 次，作为动词出现了 7 527 次），所以，学习者应该优先学习名词形式。

了解每个词的特定含义的出现频率，以及该词的搭配和它是如何跟短语结合的，也是很有用的。

在 BNC 中检索语境中的关键词 kowtow，会发现大约 14 个例子（图 8.6）。研究一下关键词索引行，可以发现这个词经常被用在否定含义里，如 refuse to kowtow（拒绝屈从）、would never kowtow（绝不顺从）、would not allow to kowtow（不许屈服），等等。

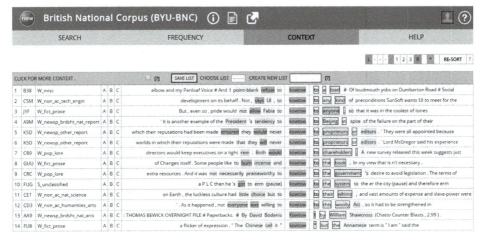

图 8.6

这些否定的用法给 MACMILLAN 词典提供了依据,其中有个标记表明这个词被用来表示不赞成、不同意(图 8.7)。kowtowing 在英语中不应该出现。

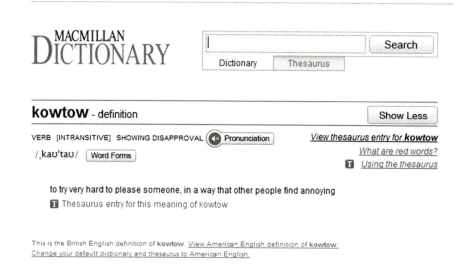

图 8.7

kowtow 这个词的定义和它在早期牛津英文词典中的词源意义以及中心意义都有所不同(早期的意义偏指用头接触地面)。关键词索引显示,在英语中,这个词更典型的意思是"尽力取悦某人"(另一层意思,其他人觉得很讨厌)。这就是中心意义和典型意义的不同,语料库语言学可以清楚地阐明这一点。

最后一个问题是如何用例证来解释词义。语料库词典学早期的理念是例证出自语料库。这个实践要追溯到塞缪尔·约翰逊(Samuel Johnson)开创性的词典,出版于 1755 年的《英语大辞典》(图 8.8)。这本词典中的例证即源于约翰逊喜欢的文学作品。比如他在解释副词 zealously 的时候用的是著名诗人约翰·弥尔顿(John Milton)的诗。

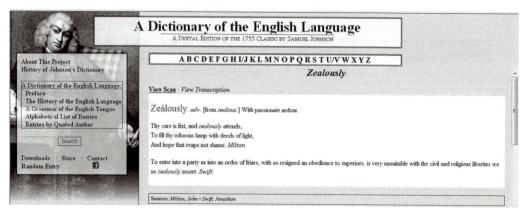

图 8.8

《剑桥国际英语词典》的编纂者批评了直接使用语料库中的例子这一做法:"大部分例证都不适合出现在学习者词典中,因为语法很复杂,含有不必要的难词和习语,有文化独立暗示或者涉及特定语境。未来的词典编纂者应该关注语料库数据,但要在数据的基础上简单、清楚地进行解释,来辅助读者学习。"

剑桥在线词典对 zealous 下定义时给出了一个短语(图 8.9),非常简单,虽然很可能也是来源于语料库中的例子,但是是经过仔细挑选的,还可能进行了简化。

图 8.9

课后拓展

试着用 BNC 语料库检索语境中的关键词 kowtow,观察一下这些例子,并查阅词典,你能发现什么?

典例示范

检索 kowtow 这个单词(图 8.10),结果有 14 个例子(图 8.11),并且大都和含有否定意义的动词或者副词连用,比如 refuse to kowtow、would not allow to kowtow、would never to kowtow、not everyone was willing to kowtow。

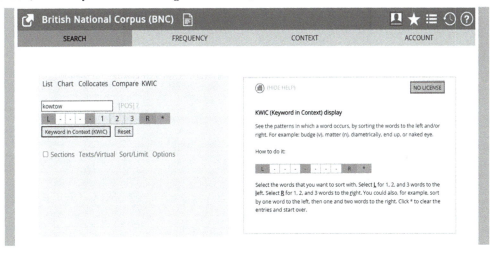

图 8.10

图 8.11

通过查阅 MACMILLAN 词典(图 8.12)可以发现,否定的意义在词典中有所体现,SHOWING DISAPPROVAL 说明语料库为词典编纂提供了依据。

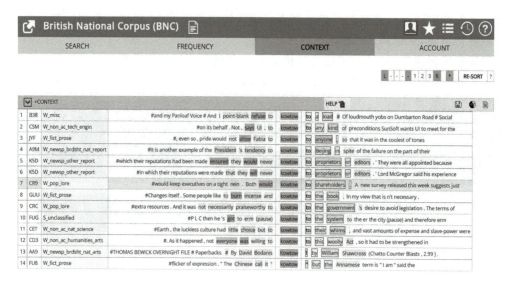

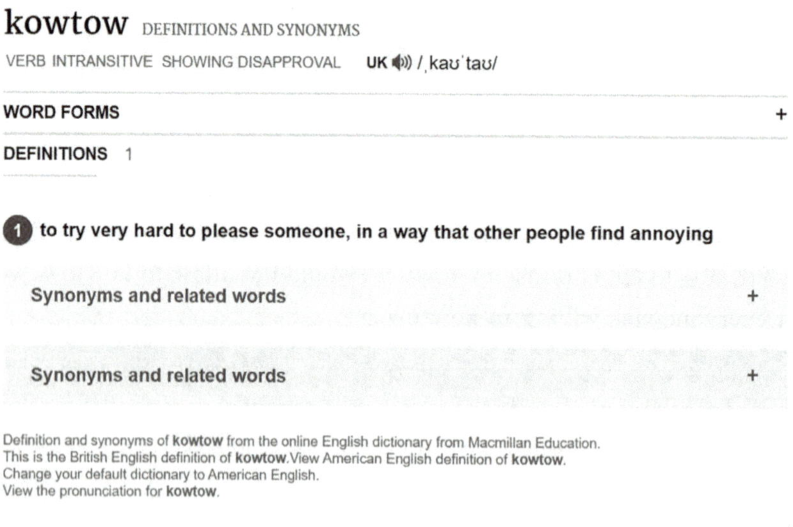

图 8.12

第九章 数据驱动语法

语料工具

- 英国国家语料库(BNC)
- 杨百翰大学语料库(BYU)
- 当代美国英语语料库(COCA)

教学内容

本章我们用语料库数据来描述语法现象。(Anderson, et al., 2017)

首先,我们来简单了解一下语言学历史。

现代语言学之父,瑞士语言学家索绪尔(Ferdinand de Saussure)界定了一些语言学里的关键概念。他区分了语言和言语。语言是存在于人类头脑中的社会心理现象,是一个整体的系统,是抽象的规则和语法;而言语指的是人们在说和写中产出的话语,是抽象规则和语法的证明。(你可能会认为,这是基本的语言方法。)索绪尔还鼓励现代语言学家思考语言的现状,共时的语言规则而不是这些规则的演变。索绪尔还区分了两种语言学关系——聚合关系(什么在话语中可以被取代,名词和代词可以取代其他名词,动词可以取代动词,诸如此类)和组合关系(诸如名词和动词组合到一起构成在语法意义上可接受的句子)。索绪尔给现代语言学家提供了研究目标(制订语言规则,并用聚合关系和组合关系构建这些规则)和方法论。

索绪尔的工作影响了欧洲一些学者的研究,像法兰兹·鲍亚士(Franz Boas)移居到美国研究人类学,主要研究正快速消亡的印第安语。语言学人种学家把语言如何发生作用应用于记录快速消亡的部落语言。他们的经验启发了布龙菲尔德(Leonard Bloomfield)的研究,布龙菲尔德的成果发表于 20 世纪 30 年代,他提出语法结构是一系列更小的成分,句子可以被分为从句、短语、单词,直到最小的语法——成分词素。

查尔斯·弗里斯(Charles Fries)发展了布龙菲尔德的理论,通过思考句子中形式的分布,他重新归纳了熟悉的词性,主要关注在英语中什么可以被代替,什么可以整合。

有两个语法理论和布龙菲尔德的相左。乔姆斯基(Avram Noam Chomsky)翻新了语法理论的目的和方法,并提出不要关注语言(这里的语言指 langue)而要关注语言运用(即个体的语法知识,如何生成可以接受的句子。)乔姆斯基的理论是革命性的,它指引着语法理论朝建构语法思维模型发展。但在引出这类数据方面语料库不是特别有用(因为本族语者仅依靠直觉就足够了),所以乔姆斯基学派不太重视语料库。

让人更容易接受的语料库语法理论学家是韩礼德(M. A. K. Halliday),他的系统功能语法使我们回想起早期在欧洲占主要地位的意义形式。韩礼德的语法理论指明语法是一套有意义的选择,有着正式的含义。比如,单数和复数之间的选择是一个有意义的选择,通常有明确的正式的含义,还有在很多语言中我们改变单数名词和复数名词的形式。对此,语料库可以提供有意义、有明显区别的证明。

约翰·辛克莱(John Sinclair),语料库语言学的先驱之一,发展了数据驱动语法的概念。在某种程度上,语料库把我们带回到索绪尔时期,让我们突然接触到言语的价值。我们能用它描述言语团所依附的语言规则吗?

很重要的一点是,不是所有的语法学家都是被数据驱动的。对于一些理论来说,直觉和一些有限的数据就足够了。语法学家需要案例用于语料库分析,选择案例的几个依据如下:①语法描述的证明是自然的,而不是基于某人的编造或偏好;②语法描述的证明基于一系列变体和体裁,不局限于语法学家自己的语言学领域;③如果一个语料库设计得很好,那么可以从中概括(例如,COCA 里有对美国英语的真实描述,包括书面语和口语);④对于语料库,如果使用得好,可以告诉我们许多以前没有注意到的模式,给我们提供一些超过正常个人直觉能力的信息。你可能会在分析语料库数据感叹:"啊,我以前居然没注意到!"

20 世纪末,《朗文英语口语和书面语语法》(*Longman Grammar of Spoken and Written English*)一书出版。请注意标题中的"口语和书面语"。随着口语语料库的发展,话语第一次被很认真地对待。十几年前,剑桥大学出版社进军教育市场,带领他们全方位指导英语语法理念的,依旧是口语和书面语(基于剑桥国际语料库,一个相当庞大的语言学来源)。朗文和剑桥语法正在改变着我们对于语言如何发生作用的理解。

现在我们来想想用语料库干什么。在语料库中我们可以探寻什么,取决于它是否对词性做了标记。如果没有,就需要注意所搜索的词或词串。例如,如果搜索情态动词 may,有可能会检索到女性的名字或月份。

如果使用的是句法标注过的语料库,那么可以做得更多。我们来看看。

首先,我们来看看用词串可以做些什么。"He is not."有两种缩写形式,"He's not."和"He isn't."。假如有人问你,哪种更常见,你该如何证明?

在 BNC 语料库中查阅一下,我们会发现这个结果是显而易见的(图 9.1):有 1894 个例子用的是"He's not.",有 372 个例子用的是"He isn't."。

还可以在其他语料库里看看检索结果,比如 TIME 或 COCA。

对比多个语料库的分析结果,还能发现这两种形式的缩写使用频率在美国和英国有一点不同:isn't 这种形式在英国的使用比率为 14%～16%,而在美国只有 2%～3%。

下面我们学习使用语法分析器,比如兰卡斯特大学的 CLAWS,如图 9.2 所示。Laurence Antony 中也有免费的语法分析器。

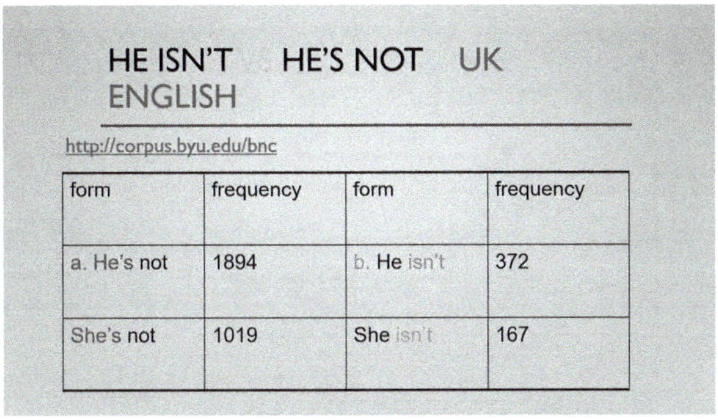

第九章 数据驱动语法

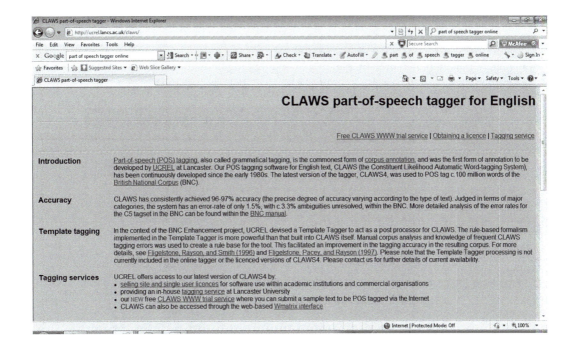

图 9.1

图 9.2

需要注意的是，每一个自动语法分析器都有自己的一套描述类别，例如，BNC 语料库倾向于将 of 和其他介词分离出来，所以它是单独标记。但并不是所有的语法学家都赞同这些描述归类。而这显然会影响检索结果。

在线练习

使用标记过的语料库可以做很多事。例如，当 over 后面跟 wh-从句时，哪些动词会出现在 over 前面？我们可以在 COCA 中检索一下，如图 9.3 所示。

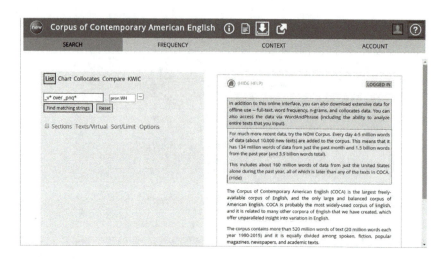

图 9.3

结果相当明确。如图 9.4 所示,可以看到一个清楚的意义结构显现出来。

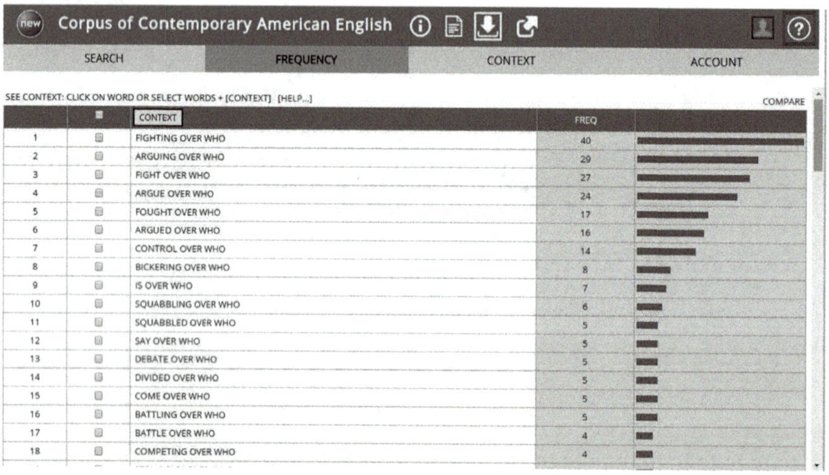

图 9.4

COCA 的检索结果证明了 Hunston 和 Francis 的分析,在结构 verb over＋wh-从句中,动词趋向于分享 argue 或 fight 的意义。这是一个有用的结构。

对于词汇,语料库给了我们很多证明聚合关系和组合关系的数据,用语法来解释语言。但我们也应该小心:语料库向我们展示了发生了什么,但没有反面证明,即不会告诉我们没有发生的。比如,能否把 all the young women 变成 the all young women,语料库不会直接给我们答案,而本族语者会。语料库可能被曲解——这取决于它的设计。即使是 COCA 的口语语料部分,也被误解为不用稿子的媒体话语。语料库提供数据但是没有解释——数据不是它自己的描述,而这是我们要做的。并非所有的语料库都适合所有的问题。语料库可以帮助我们研究在真实使用中的语法,而不是教师或语言学家所想的,应该怎么用,可以怎么用。

语料库的强大之处在于它能让我们接触自然语料，远远超过本族语者的直觉。这里有一个关注点言语，用话语表达，以及语言的社会功能，更多涉及认知。这是语法研究的核心（自 20 世纪 60 年代起）。简而言之，数据驱动语法意味着回归语法分析的社会功能，用来解释社会群体的话语模式，而不是提出语法知识的思维模型。随着语料库语言学的发展，社会学和认知之间的鸿沟将会被填补。

课后拓展

请分别用 BNC 和 COCA 语料库检索当 over 后面跟 wh-从句时，over 前面分别跟着什么动词。比较两个语料库的检索结果并加以阐释。

典例示范

BNC 的检索结果如图 9.5 所示，频繁出现的前十个结构为 squabbling over who、arguing over who、argue over who、voice over whoever、voice over who、take over who、swither over who、split over who、sniggering over who、quarreled over who。

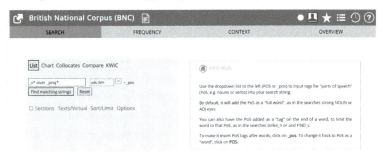

(a)

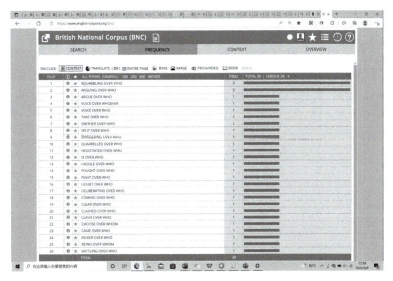

(b)

图 9.5

而在 COCA 中频繁出现的结构有 fighting over who、arguing over who、fight over who、argue over who、argued over who、fought over who、control over who、is over who、bickering over who、competing over who 等，如图 9.6 所示。

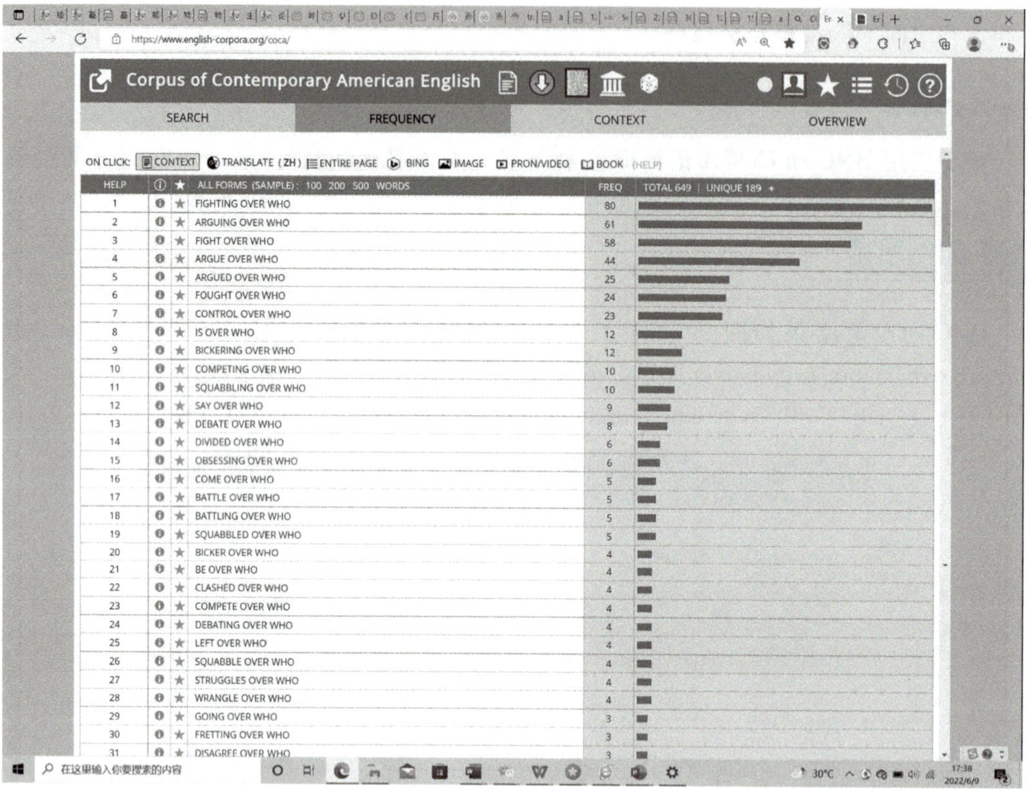

HELP	ALL FORMS (SAMPLE)	FREQ
1	FIGHTING OVER WHO	80
2	ARGUING OVER WHO	61
3	FIGHT OVER WHO	58
4	ARGUE OVER WHO	44
5	ARGUED OVER WHO	25
6	FOUGHT OVER WHO	24
7	CONTROL OVER WHO	23
8	IS OVER WHO	12
9	BICKERING OVER WHO	12
10	COMPETING OVER WHO	10
11	SQUABBLING OVER WHO	10
12	SAY OVER WHO	9
13	DEBATE OVER WHO	8
14	DIVIDED OVER WHO	6
15	OBSESSING OVER WHO	6
16	COME OVER WHO	5
17	BATTLE OVER WHO	5
18	BATTLING OVER WHO	5
19	SQUABBLED OVER WHO	5
20	BICKER OVER WHO	4
21	BE OVER WHO	4
22	CLASHED OVER WHO	4
23	COMPETE OVER WHO	4
24	DEBATING OVER WHO	4
25	LEFT OVER WHO	4
26	SQUABBLE OVER WHO	4
27	STRUGGLES OVER WHO	4
28	WRANGLE OVER WHO	4
29	GOING OVER WHO	3
30	FRETTING OVER WHO	3
31	DISAGREE OVER WHO	3

图 9.6

虽然两个语料库的检索结果表明英式英语和美式英语在使用上存在一些差异(出现频率最高的结构不太一样)，但是这些词基本上都是与“争吵”这个意思有关，因此我们可以得出over后跟 wh-从句时，前面的动词通常都是与 fight、argue 等意思相近的动词。

第⑩章　话语标记语 听者身份 关系语言

📝 语料工具

- ●当代美国英语语料库(COCA)
- ●苏格兰英语语料库(SCOTS)
- ●杨百翰大学语料库(BYU)

📖 教学内容

本章来看看口语语料库,它是新近在语料库语言学中发展起来的。我们将会特别关注那些在口语中出现频率异常的语言学特点,并判断这些特点是如何处理说话人和听话人之间的关系的。

先看看口语语料库中的话语标记语,想想它们在对话共建中的角色,想想作为听者身份的语言本质。实际上,我们在考虑的是对话语言如何处理交际双方的关系。

话语标记语是语言学中很有意思的特点,但很容易被忽视,因为虽然它们用得很多,但通常有很多意思。这些词诸如 ok、right、yeah、well、so、anyway、you know,还有些长一点的,像 you know what I mean 和 at the end of the day。是什么让这些表达能够被认为是话语标记语呢?有一个线索是这些表达的分布。语料库证据显示这些表达在口语中出现的频率高于书面语。

✏️ 在线练习1

在 COCA 中查看 right(图 10.1)或 at the end of the day(图 10.2)的图表分析结果,可以发现这些表达毫无疑问地出现在书面写作中,但是它们在口语中出现得更加频繁。这些表达在口语中的出现频率表明它们在口语中有特定的功能,而这些功能在书面语中并不具备。

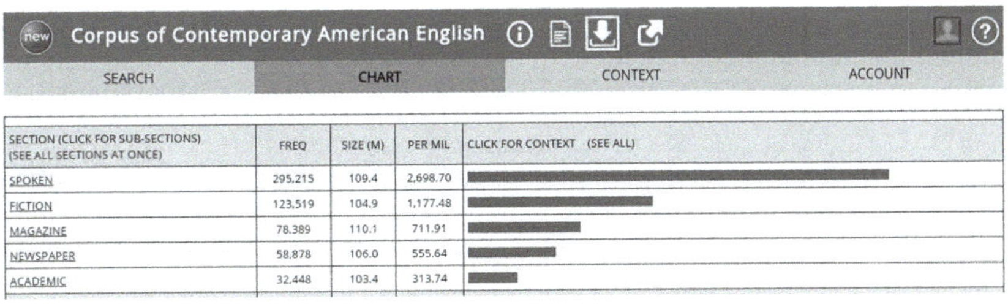

SECTION (CLICK FOR SUB-SECTIONS) (SEE ALL SECTIONS AT ONCE)	FREQ	SIZE (M)	PER MIL	CLICK FOR CONTEXT (SEE ALL)
SPOKEN	295,215	109.4	2,698.70	
FICTION	123,519	104.9	1,177.48	
MAGAZINE	78,389	110.1	711.59	
NEWSPAPER	58,878	106.0	555.64	
ACADEMIC	32,448	103.4	313.74	

图 10.1

SECTION (CLICK FOR SUB-SECTIONS) (SEE ALL SECTIONS AT ONCE)	FREQ	SIZE (M)	PER MIL	CLICK FOR CONTEXT (SEE ALL)
SPOKEN	1,977	109.4	18.07	
FICTION	376	104.9	3.58	
MAGAZINE	720	110.1	6.54	
NEWSPAPER	718	106.0	6.78	
ACADEMIC	193	103.4	1.87	

图 10.2

通过观察发现，话语标记语经常出现在回答某人的问题中。应答标记在语言学中被赋予各种各样的名字：back-channeling（反馈信号）、minimal and non-minimal responses（最小和非最小回应）、listener response（听者回应）。最小回应通常是简短的话语，经常是一两个音节的长度，像 ok、mmhm、yeah，或只扬扬眉毛。取决于你的语料库，这些特征可能也可能不会被解码或标记。非最小回应有很多，可以是副词（像 totally）或形容词（像 like），或者长一点的短语（像 is that so? 或 is that right?）。

通过观察口语语料库的文字转录，你可以看到这些是如何发生作用的。下面的对话来源于苏格兰语料库。在这一对话中，说话人 M642 在讲述摩托车锦标赛；而听话人的回应标记，像 uh、huh、aye，或是大笑。

> F643：That's the Boys' Own picture of //Stevie,//
>
> M642：//Steve// Hislop, British Superbike Motorcycle Champion this year.
>
> M608：oh right?
>
> M642：And, that's er, he was down at North Harbour Motorcycles
>
> M608：uh-huh
>
> M642：and that's his 'weeHizzy helmet'.
>
> M608：huh
>
> M642：//He's got//
>
> F643：//[laugh]//
>
> M642：the wee dervish Scottish cycle, kind of, it it's almost like the erm Tasmanian Devil,
>
> M608：Aye.
>
> M642：but in a kilt.

非最小回应标记在不同的对话中，包括 right、oh right。如下面这段对话中，两个学生在讨论论文题目。

> F745: Okay, erm so, what's your dissertation about?
> F746: erm, I actually did mine on Onomastics, //like,//
> F745: //Right.//
> F746: about, yeah, about kind of, oh God, [inhale] aye, the additional names that people use in my island; the kind of system of naming.
> F745: oh right, what what isl-island is it you come from?
> F746: North Uist,
> F745: Right.
> F746: in the Western Isles, I don't know if you know where that //is. [laugh]//

有时候这些回应标记成群或成串出现在说话人的口语表达中。在下面这段对话里我们看到三个最小回应标记依次出现：uh-huh、yeah、mmhm。

> M642: I was born in, s-s-t-, no, not sou-, my sister was born in South Lodge.
> M608: mmhm
> M642: I was at Invercar,
> M608: mmhm
> M642: which I think it just off, Invercar was just off Castlehill Road.
> F643: uh-huh yeah. Mmhm

要了解这些特征是如何形成的十分困难。Carter 和 McCarthy 都曾表示回应标记成串出现发生在话题的边界（O'Keeffe, et al., 2007），但仅从苏格兰语料库中我们发现，这个观点很难被证实。

不过我们还是可以认定回应标记，并使用语料库找到哪些回应标记在口语中最普遍。McCarthy 和 Carter 列出了英语中 19 个使用最普遍的非最小回应标记，如图 10.3 所示，这些常见的表达在对话中出现得很频繁。你能在口语中正确使用这些表达吗？

Most common non-minimal responses in US/UK English

1-10	11-20
Really	Absolutely
Right	Certainly
Good	wonderful
Quite	Lovely
Great	Definitely
True	Gosh
Sure	Cool
Exactly	Excellent
Fine	Perfect
Wow	

图 10.3

要想有效地使用回应标记，首先需要看看回应标记的作用。话语分析表明，回应标记有四个主要的功能：①表示说话人可以继续说话，说话人在讲话，听话人只说 mmhm 或其他类似表达。②表示同意说话人的话，这种标记叫做趋同标记，比如 yeah、I know、sure、totally，或只是重复说话人刚说过的话。③表达热情或同感，或者惊讶、震惊，比如 aww、no!、you are kidding 等。④特定情景下的反应，比如确认跟某人的约会安排(fine with me，我没问题)，或同意服务请求(certainly sir 或 right away, madam)，等等。

在线练习 2

用苏格兰语料库的高级搜索来看看标记语的使用。在单词检索框中键入 uh-huh，然后设置 Document details 为 Spoken，如图 10.4 所示。

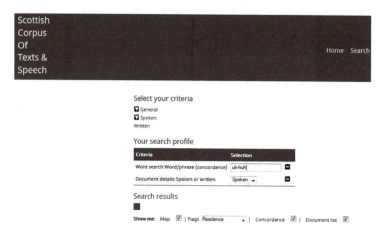

图 10.4

可以看到最小回应标记的关键词索引(图 10.5)，看看它们的功能，是不是说话人要继续或者表达同意？我们可以回到文字转录看看这些表达的语境。

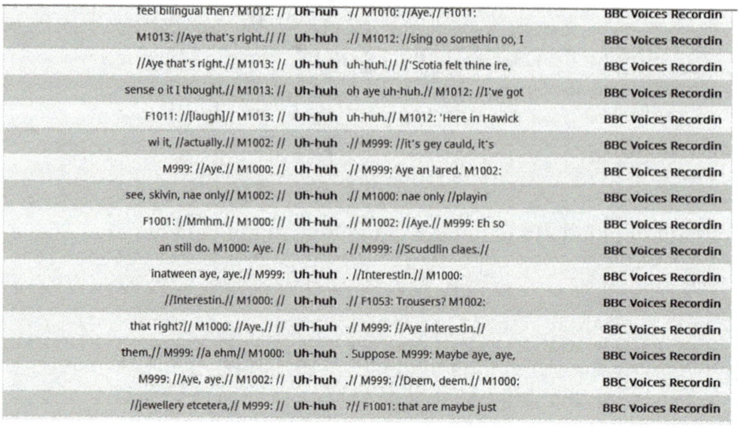

feel bilingual then? M1012: //	Uh-huh	.// M1010: //Aye.// F1011:	BBC Voices Recordin
M1013: //Aye that's right.// //	Uh-huh	.// M1012: //sing oo somethin oo, I	BBC Voices Recordin
//Aye that's right.// M1013: //	Uh-huh	uh-huh.// //'Scotia felt thine ire,	BBC Voices Recordin
sense o it I thought.// M1013: //	Uh-huh	oh aye uh-huh.// M1012: //I've got	BBC Voices Recordin
F1011: //[laugh]// M1013: //	Uh-huh	uh-huh.// M1012: 'Here in Hawick	BBC Voices Recordin
wi it, //actually.// M1002: //	Uh-huh	.// M999: //it's gey cauld, it's	BBC Voices Recordin
M999: //Aye.// M1000: //	Uh-huh	.// M999: Aye an lared. M1002:	BBC Voices Recordin
see, skivin, nae only// M1002: //	Uh-huh	.// M1000: nae only //playin	BBC Voices Recordin
F1001: //Mmhm.// M1000: //	Uh-huh	.// M1002: //Aye.// M999: Eh so	BBC Voices Recordin
an still do. M1000: Aye. //	Uh-huh	.// M999: //Scuddlin claes.//	BBC Voices Recordin
inatween aye, aye.// M999:	Uh-huh	. //Interestin.// M1000:	BBC Voices Recordin
//Interestin.// M1000: //	Uh-huh	.// F1053: Trousers? M1002:	BBC Voices Recordin
that right?// M1000: //Aye.// //	Uh-huh	.// M999: //Aye interestin.//	BBC Voices Recordin
them.// M999: //a ehm// M1000:	Uh-huh	. Suppose. M999: Maybe aye, aye,	BBC Voices Recordin
M999: //Aye, aye.// M1002: //	Uh-huh	.// M999: //Deem, deem.// M1000:	BBC Voices Recordin
//jewellery etcetera,// M999: //	Uh-huh	?// F1001: that are maybe just	BBC Voices Recordin

图 10.5

有一个趋同标记是 totally,经常单独出现在话语中。

介入标记包括笑和表示同情的声音 aw。

在口语里不经常出现的表达和书面语相比如何呢?它们的功能有点像话语标记语。话语标记语的功能包括组织话语结构,通过打开或关闭一系列信息的信号来产生话题边界,转换、回溯或聚焦。

其他的话语标记语被用来监控话语,通过重组那些没有被理解或没有说清楚的信息,又或是那些要分享的信息。

研究最多的方面是立场的探究,即话语标记语是如何发出信号让人感受到某些东西的。如 actually 指事实,I must say 表示强调观点,I'm afraid 表示承认说话人和听话人之间的立场有分歧,等等。在口语中,说话人试图避免正面回答或者弱化他们的观点,常使用诸如 kind of、sort of 这样的表达。这些话语标记语帮助人们处理关系,保留面子。关于语言学中的礼貌性经常会讨论这些。

在线练习 3

要明白表达是如何发生作用的,需要深挖这些数据。比如 BNC 和 COCA 告诉我们 are you sure 作为短语在口语和小说中使用很频繁(图 10.6)。数据告诉我们 are you sure 在口语中有特定功能,这些功能是什么呢?

British National Corpus (BYU-BNC)

SEARCH | CHART | CONTEXT | HELP

SECTION (CLICK FOR SUB-SECTIONS) (SEE ALL SECTIONS AT ONCE)	FREQ	SIZE (M)	PER MIL	CLICK FOR CONTEXT (SEE ALL)
SPOKEN	208	10.0	20.88	
FICTION	417	15.9	26.21	
MAGAZINE	15	7.3	2.07	
NEWSPAPER	2	10.5	0.19	
NON-ACAD	4	16.5	0.24	
ACADEMIC	2	15.3	0.13	
MISC	62	20.8	2.98	
TOTAL	710			SEE ALL TOKENS

(a)

Corpus of Contemporary American English

SEARCH | CHART | CONTEXT | ACCOUNT

SECTION (CLICK FOR SUB-SECTIONS) (SEE ALL SECTIONS)	FREQ	SIZE (M)	PER MIL	CLICK FOR CONTEXT (SEE ALL)
SPOKEN	429	109.4	3.92	
FICTION	1,704	104.9	16.24	
MAGAZINE	158	110.1	1.43	
NEWSPAPER	83	106.0	0.78	
ACADEMIC	31	103.4	0.30	
1990-1994	427	104.0	4.11	
1995-1999	420	103.4	4.06	
2000-2004	440	102.9	4.27	
2005-2009	503	102.0	4.93	
2010-2015	615	121.6	5.06	
TOTAL	4,810			SEE ALL TOKENS

(b)

图 10.6

我们来看一些来自 COCA 的典型例子：①提出邀请；②礼貌拒绝；③第一个说话人问 are you sure 进行核实并再次邀请；④第二个说话人确认拒绝或接受再次邀请；⑤第一个说话人认可或评估接受程度。

这种情节在英语中很常见。McCarthy 和 Carter 把 are you sure 称为承诺言语行为，它让某人在不丢面子的情况下接受或拒绝邀请。

话语标记语告诉我们如何处理对话，以及如何处理对话双方的关系。想想下面几个问题：①本族语者和非本族语者使用话语标记语的方式一样吗？从一语转到二语是否容易？在这一点上，学习者要被教授吗？②话语标记语在不同语境中的使用方式也不同吗？例如在非本族语者的口语中或在不同口语题材，如商务会谈或者讲座中，又或者是将英语作为通用语的情况下。③如果要在英语课堂中明确地教非本族语者使用这些标记语，如何教会他们呢？

课后拓展

1. Use BNC and COCA to search for the context where "are you sure" appears. What are your findings? Describe based on the content you learned in class.

典例示范

Discourse markers are essential to manage the flow and structure of discourse, the meanings of which cannot always be found in the dictionary we use. However, they do have certain functions and convey specific indications as a way to help us communicate with people. They can be used to start or end a topic, indicate shared knowledge between speakers, show our attitude, response to others, etc.

The total frequency of "are you sure" in COCA is 13427 times.（图 10.7）Most of them were used in the TV/M, and the raw frequency is 10025 times. "Are you sure" was used most frequently between 2015 to 2019. Examples can be seen in the following pictures.（图 10.8）

SECTION	ALL	BLOG	WEB	TV/M	SPOK	FIC	MAG	NEWS	ACAD	1990-94	1995-99	2000-04	2005-09	2010-14	2015-19
FREQ	13427	323	331	10025	492	1961	168	91	36	1719	2239	2234	2100	2217	2264
WORDS (M)	993	128.6	124.3	128.1	126.1	118.3	126.1	121.7	119.8	139.1	147.8	146.6	144.9	145.3	144.7
PER MIL	13.52	2.51	2.66	78.27	3.90	16.57	1.33	0.75	0.30	12.36	15.15	15.24	14.49	15.26	15.64

图 10.7

CLICK FOR MORE CONTEXT　EXPLORE NEW FEATURES　SAVE　TRANSLATE　ANALYZE

1	2019	TV	Arrested Development	debt. Oh, God, I just got an amiable nod. **Are you sure** it was amiable? Yeah, it was pretty amiable. Okay, look away
2	2019	TV	Arrested Development	all a little stressed right now, being stuck in this attic. **Are you sure** we can't just live downstairs in the real house? Oh, this is
3	2019	TV	Divorce	. I'm gon na swing by a couple of job sites. **Are you sure** you're gon na be okay on the Dick Cheney torture bed? Oh,
4	2019	TV	This Is Us	. Tell him the one that he likes is in aisle four. **Are you sure**?' Cause I don't mind you having your day. I'm sure
5	2019	TV	This Is Us	late, so maybe you should just meet me at the party. **Are you sure**? Yeah, just-just meet me there. I'll text you the address on
6	2019	TV	This Is Us	, Randall. Thanks for dropping me off, Mom. Kate, **are you sure** about this? Yeah. Just-just come to our graduation. You're gon na
7	2019	TV	This Is Us	life with kids, it's no contest. I choose you. **Are you sure**? Really sure? If you need more time... I choose you. (m It
8	2019	TV	This Is Us	and little Tobe deserve some local Grandpa and Grandma time, too. **Are you sure** you guys are gon na be okay with everything? Of course. We al
9	2019	TV	This Is Us	I feel like I need some caffeine. Do you want anything? **Are you sure**? Mm. Okay. I'm proud of you, cuz. I know
10	2019	TV	The Big Bang Theory	scientific word for dust. What was wrong with " dust "? **Are you sure** you're not just a little jealous? No. It's just, my
11	2019	TV	The Big Bang Theory	feel so alone. Wow. That is quite the guilt trip. **Are you sure** you're not Jewish? I'm just a wife that is so proud of
12	2019	TV	The Big Bang Theory	a question? Yeah. Actually, I have a two-part question. **Are you sure**? I get the sense it's only one part. No, no,
13	2019	TV	The Big Bang Theory	a thesis? " Well, plagiarism is a pretty serious charge. **Are you sure**? You want proof? I can make some calls. You'd do that
14	2019	TV	The OA	for her. Everyone has their limits. I need her back. **Are you sure** that's best? Hunter. (knocking-on-door What I'm saying is... uh, maybe
15	2019	TV	Good Omens	what you smell like. The Hell Hound has found its master. **Are you sure**? I felt it. Would I lie to you? Well, obviously.
16	2019	TV	True Detective	be best for both of us you didn't mention this exchange. **Are you sure** you're not trying to investigate this again? That'd be a job for
17	2019	TV	Shadowhunters	'm coming with you. No. I need to be alone. **Are you sure** this is gon na work? Nora Kendall's the one who gave Jordan the
18	2019	TV	Shadowhunters	. Every demon has their weakness. What's hers? Me. **Are you sure** that's where you want to summon her? An abandoned power plant? It

(a)TV /Movies

CLICK FOR MORE CONTEXT　EXPLORE NEW FEATURES　SAVE　TRANSLATE　ANALYZE

1	2019	FIC	SciFi & Fantasy	gives True the key and slips out of the house soundlessly. # " **Are you sure**? " True says to Jamie and Liv. # Jamie laughs. " No
2	2019	FIC	SciFi & Fantasy	could sneak in the back and get her out? " # " **Are you sure**? " True says. # " Are you? " Bess retorts. # "
3	2019	FIC	The Maine Review	-- drove her to the Point Reyes Inn at around I A.M. " **Are you sure** there's nothing I can get for you? Toothbrush? Aspirin? " he
4	2019	FIC	Azalea	. " # She looked at me gravely and asked again, " **Are you sure**? " # " I mean, was it a few months ago? But
5	2019	FIC	Azalea	this the other day when we met up. That's weird. **Are you sure** it was Sun-mi? " # " No, I don't think so.
6	2019	FIC	AntiochRev	a woman, she'll sometimes try to make eye contact, like **are you sure** you don't want a real drink? I'll try to respond with a
7	2019	FIC	The Carolina Quarterly	her forearms on the table and was leaning on them. # " **Are you sure**? " Mom asked. # " Yeah, " Amy said. # "
8	2019	FIC	The Carolina Quarterly	sort of way. " # Lena put down her wineglass. " **Are you sure** it was his house? " # " Obviously, who else's? "
9	2019	FIC	War Lit Arts	. They'll put you where they need you. " # " **Are you sure**? " # " They will take care of you. You will get to
10	2019	FIC	SciFi & Fantasy	, right? " # " Of course not. " # " **Are you sure**? " # Around the Epitaph Incorporated office, they called it cybercide. # It
11	2019	FIC	Subtropics	! " She pointed to the bag of sandwiches between them. " **Are you sure** you don't want any? Hattie made more than enough. " # Noah
12	2019	FIC	Ploughshares	Where would she go? " # Alan turns to June. " **Are you sure** she didn't say anything to you? " " She probably wasn't feeling
13	2019	FIC	Ploughshares	# " Nothing. " # But something is. " Monica, **are you sure**? " # " What did you mean when you said,' it's
14	2019	FIC	NewEnglandRev	If you squeeze the rubber ball, we will ask you,' **Are you sure** you wanted to squeeze the rubber ball?' And if you squeeze it again
15	2019	FIC	AMASS	a short while. I don't remember ever seeing you here. **Are you sure** you have the right place? " here before and something bad happened. "
16	2019	FIC	SouthernRev	" # Mariela looked at her, suddenly completely lucid. # " **Are you sure**? " # " I thought it out. I'll take a lot of
17	2019	FIC	NewYorker	and even Carly, on dropping her off, had asked, " **Are you sure** this is the correct destination? " But they didn't know Keystone the way
18	2019	FIC	SciFi & Fantasy	. " # " The survey can take an hour or more. **Are you sure**? " # " I'll take a bottle of water, then. "

(b)Fiction

图 10.8

In BNC, "are you sure" is used 710 times in total. (图 10.9) Among these uses, fiction has 417 times and spoken language has 208 times. For example, "Are you sure? I mean, don't you…" In this sentence, "are you sure" was used to express uncertainty or questions. More examples can be seen in the following pictures. (图 10.10)

In total, "are you sure" is used frequently in daily life for questions, uncertainty, astonishment, and so on.

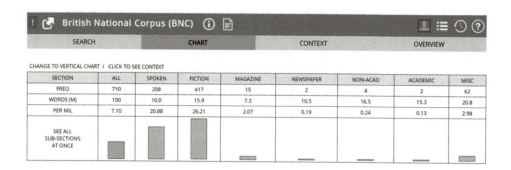

图 10.9

(a) Fiction

(b) Spoken

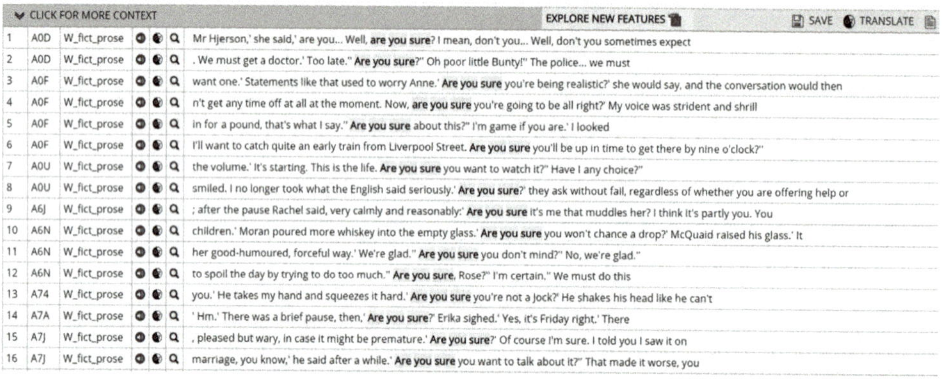

图 10.10

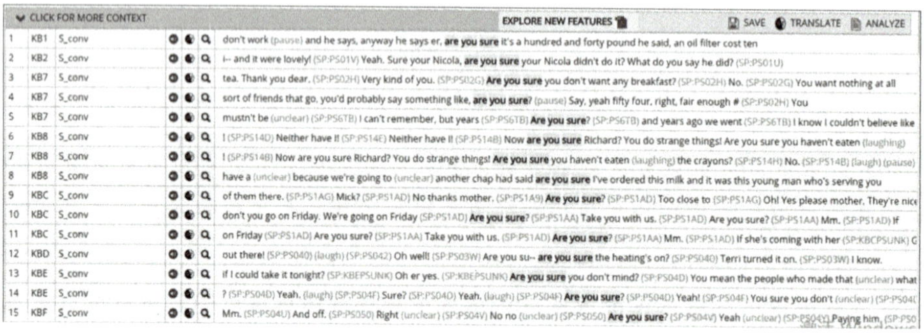

From the charts we've obtained in both corpora, obviously, "are you sure" is much more frequently used in spoken language than written language. The results show that this sentence has some certain functions in conversations, which isn't included in the dictionary. In BNC, the use in fiction, especially in prose, has the highest frequency, as there are plenty of conversations and "are you sure" can often be seen in the direct speech. In COCA, the use of "are you sure" in TV and movies is the most frequent. On the contrary, "are you sure" is seldom seen in newspapers, magazines or academic papers, as they are more formal.

Discourse markers like this also help promote interaction between speakers.

Examples from BNC:

a. Just making that one up? (SP:PS0JB) No, we are not (SP:PS0JA) Are you sure about that? (SP:PS0JB) Of course mum, mum I know.

The speaker is seeking clarification or approval to take further action.

b. Do you mind if I have a cigarette? (SP:PS6NM) No go ahead (SP:PS6NT) Are you sure? (SP:PS6NM) Go ahead I don't, no I don't mind people smoking.

The speaker uses "are you sure" to ask for permissions and confirm that others don't mind his smoking. In this way, he does without the loss of face.

Examples from COCA:

a. She wiped roughly at her cheeks. ♯ "Are you sure you should keep her? Really sure?" he asked, stricken.

The man in this situation is clearly confirming the woman's intention. "Are you sure" offers him an unoffensive way to show he wants to refuse it.

b. "Very funny." I said. " Listen: Are you sure you're all right and don't need any help?" The speaker is making an offer to help the hearer.

Maybe he has made an offer previously and now he is making a re-offer. He uses "are you sure" to avoid the loss of face. In conclusion, "are you sure" plays a role in clarifying or confirming something, making offers or requests.

According to McCarthy and Carter, "are you sure" is a kind of commissive speech that people often say to make an offer. It's an effective way to save the negative face of the hearer by allowing him to accept of refuse the offer without losing face.

2. Use BNC to search the discourse marker "actually" and describe your finds.

After searching for the discourse marker "actually" in BNC, we find out that this word occurs in spoken texts most frequently. They are from some meetings or some interviews and some conversations.

Examples from BNC:

a. toxin is not part of the genome of (pause) Cherani bacteria diphtheria, it's actually a farged mediated toxin, it's **actually** encoded for by a bacteria farged.

b. (pause) Cherani bacteria diphtheria, it's **actually** a farged mediated toxin, it's actually encoded for by a bacteria farged. So when? (SP:F8SPSUNK) What's paresis then?

c. Rapidly, within macrophages (pause) and (pause) after er (pause) a period of time is **actually** disseminated into the circulation. Now, this happens in nearly all (pause) er (pause)

d. But it's believed that the majority of cases of tuberculosis, that we **actually** see, are so called post-primary tuberculosis where all of this process is taking place

e. written T T X, which comes from a Japanese Puffer Fish. It's **actually** a er erm Japanese delicacy. You have to make sure you've removed the

f. the third one F three. Okay. Once you've done that what we **actually** do is to look for for sub-patterns in those tuples. Of course we've

g. one not X two not X three and I think on your examples you've **actually** got them labelled. Erm which means that each one of those is off.

h. whether you can (unclear) (SP:JP6PSUNK) (sneeze) (SP:PS4H3) these tuples again. So here we'd **actually** have a match of all three saying that we've recognized it to a level

i. all it does is record the binary pattern er under that area. We've **actually** taken three measurement areas. One here one in the middle one at the bottom

j. the previous page. Same as these terms here except. So the decoders are **actually** listing all the possible terms of the inputs. The memory cells here of course

k. us our response of well two maybe in this particular case. And if it **actually** recognized it. Okay so we can implement it like that in hardware but the

l. some packages made but unfortunately he didn't patent the idea (laugh) because what he **actually** was made what he actually made was random access memories. Erm and had he

m. he didn't patent the idea (laugh) because what he **actually** was made what he actually made was random access memories. Erm and had he had he patented it or

"Actually" is used very frequently in spoken language than our think. (图 10.11) It is often used as a discourse marker or a common shortcut people use to correct someone or to emphasize something. First and foremost, this word means "in fact" as an adverb, often used when a speaker wants to present a contrast from what people think or believe. For example, when A talks with B, A speaks something he/she believes to be true, but B thinks that saying is wrong, B would say: “Actually, it’s like this…” So “actually” here can be seen as a sign that you gonna correct somebody. And secondly, this word is used to emphasize something, if you want to emphasize something to be wrong, it is a good marker to do this function. And thirdly, it is used to elicit something unexpected. Examples: it takes me an hour to drive to work, although the actual distance is only 20 miles. (图 10.12—图 10.13)

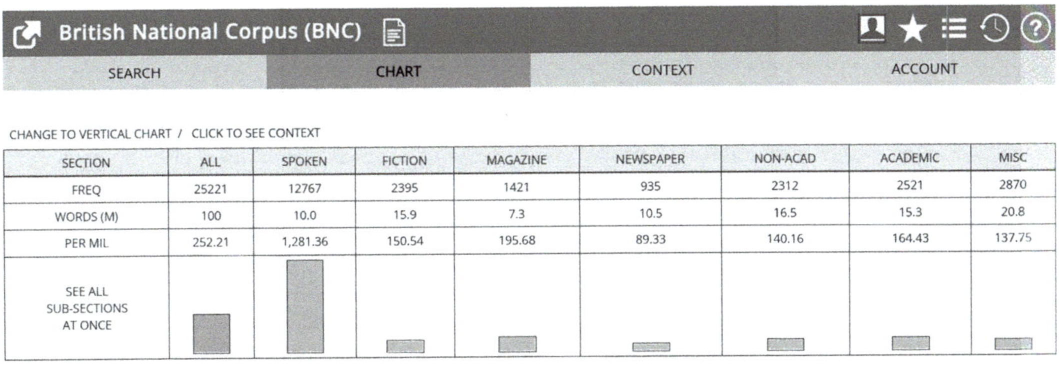

SECTION	ALL	SPOKEN	FICTION	MAGAZINE	NEWSPAPER	NON-ACAD	ACADEMIC	MISC
FREQ	25221	12767	2395	1421	935	2312	2521	2870
WORDS (M)	100	10.0	15.9	7.3	10.5	16.5	15.3	20.8
PER MIL	252.21	1,281.36	150.54	195.68	89.33	140.16	164.43	137.75
SEE ALL SUB-SECTIONS AT ONCE								

图 10.11

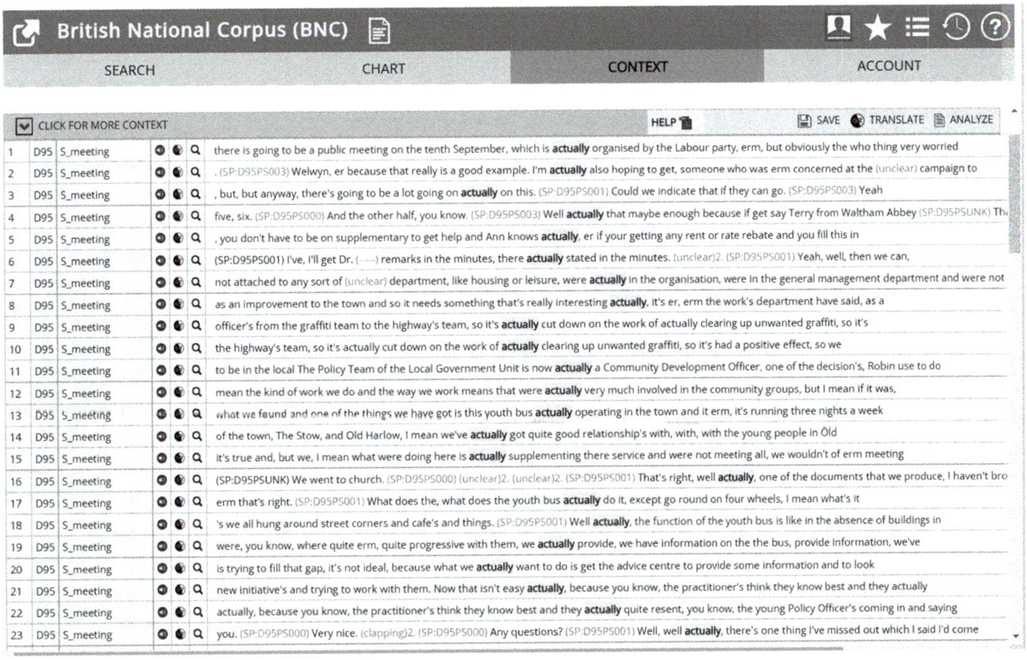

1	D95	S_meeting	there is going to be a public meeting on the tenth September, which is **actually** organised by the Labour party, erm, but obviously the who thing very worried
2	D95	S_meeting	. (SP:D95PS003) Welwyn, er because that really is a good example. I'm **actually** also hoping to get, someone who was erm concerned at the (unclear) campaign to
3	D95	S_meeting	, but, but anyway, there's going to be a lot going on **actually** on this. (SP:D95PS001) Could we indicate that if they can go. (SP:D95PS003) Yeah
4	D95	S_meeting	five, six. (SP:D95PS000) And the other half, you know. (SP:D95PS003) Well **actually** that maybe enough because if get say Terry from Waltham Abbey (SP:D95PSUNK) Th
5	D95	S_meeting	, you don't have to be on supplementary to get help and Ann knows **actually**, er if your getting any rent or rate rebate and you fill this in
6	D95	S_meeting	(SP:D95PS001) I've, I'll get Dr. (-----) remarks in the minutes, there **actually** stated in the minutes. (unclear)2. (SP:D95PS001) Yeah, well, then we can,
7	D95	S_meeting	not attached to any sort of (unclear) department, like housing or leisure, were **actually** in the organisation, were in the general management department and were not
8	D95	S_meeting	as an improvement to the town and so it needs something that's really interesting **actually**, it's er, erm the work's department have said, as a
9	D95	S_meeting	officer's from the graffiti team to the highway's team, so it's **actually** cut down on the work of actually clearing up unwanted graffiti, so it's
10	D95	S_meeting	the highway's team, so it's actually cut down on the work of **actually** clearing up unwanted graffiti, so it's had a positive effect, so we
11	D95	S_meeting	to be in the local The Policy Team of the Local Government Unit is now **actually** a Community Development Officer, one of the decision's, Robin use to do
12	D95	S_meeting	mean the kind of work we do and the way we work means that were **actually** very much involved in the community groups, but I mean if it was,
13	D95	S_meeting	what we found and one of the things we have got is this youth bus **actually** operating in the town and it erm, it's running three nights a week
14	D95	S_meeting	of the town, The Stow, and Old Harlow, I mean we've **actually** got quite good relationship's with, with, with the young people in Old
15	D95	S_meeting	it's true and, but we, I mean what were doing here is **actually** supplementing there service and were not meeting all, we wouldn't of erm meeting
16	D95	S_meeting	(SP:D95PSUNK) We went to church. (SP:D95PS000) (unclear)2. (unclear)2. (SP:D95PS001) That's right, well **actually**, one of the documents that we produce, I haven't bro
17	D95	S_meeting	erm that's right. (SP:D95PS001) What does the, what does the youth bus **actually** do it, except go round on four wheels, I mean what's it
18	D95	S_meeting	's we all hung around street corners and cafe's and things. (SP:D95PS001) Well **actually**, the function of the youth bus is like in the absence of buildings in
19	D95	S_meeting	were, you know, where quite erm, quite progressive with them, we **actually** provide, we have information on the the bus, provide information, we've
20	D95	S_meeting	is trying to fill that gap, it's not ideal, because what we **actually** want to do is get the advice centre to provide some information and to look
21	D95	S_meeting	new initiative's and trying to work with them. Now that isn't easy **actually**, because you know, the practitioner's think they know best and they actually
22	D95	S_meeting	actually, because you know, the practitioner's think they know best and they **actually** quite resent, you know, the young Policy Officer's coming in and saying
23	D95	S_meeting	you. (SP:D95PS000) Very nice. (clapping)2. (SP:D95PS000) Any questions? (SP:D95PS001) Well, well **actually**, there's one thing I've missed out which I said I'd come

图 10.12

图 10.13

第十一章 语言变体

📝 语料工具

- ●当代美国英语语料库（COCA）
- ●苏格兰文本口语语料库

📖 教学内容

本章学习语料库和语言变体。

我们简要地看看两种变体：在标准语言中的变体[依据情境（通常指我们所说的语域），依据交际目的（也就是我们说的体裁）和依据个人美学选择（即我们所说的风格）]，以及语料库语言学较少涉及的地理变体（就是英式英语、美式英语、印度英语、澳大利亚英语间的不同，或在英国、美国、印度等国家不同地区所说英语的不同）。这方面的内容可参考 Wendy Anderson 和 John Corbett 所著的 *Exploring English with Online Corpora*（包括了语言变体的讨论），以及 Douglas Biber 和 Susan Conrad 所著的 *Register, Genre, and Style*；Tony McEnery、Richard Xiao 和 Yukio Tono 的著作 *Corpus-based Language Studies* 中也有相关内容。

很多大的语料库都是建立在标准英语的基础上的，趋向于在编辑词典、语法中使用。而近些年各种非标准变体（苏格兰英语、爱尔兰英语，学习者语料库和 ELF 语料库）都有所发展，通常比较小，并包含口语数据。

下面看看使用标准变体语料库和非标准变体语料库探索语言变体的方法。我们从标准语言变体开始。

标准语言变体经常用三个易混淆但很明确的词来描述——语域、体裁、风格。

语域是指依据语境而产生的变体：在随意的闲聊中所使用的语言和在商务会议中所使用的语言不同，也和报纸中足球报道使用的语言不同。大的在线语料库（像 COCA 或 BNC）让我们能看到英语的不同语域，例如学术英语和小说中的英语，或杂志中的英语和英语口语。我们可以看到词汇和特定结构在每个语域中的分布。

体裁是指依据交际目的而产生的变体，例如，一篇学术研究文章可能因杂志宣传而具有不同的目的。体裁分析通常考虑文本或话语的整体框架是如何构建的，以此方式来实现交际目的。体裁分析把这些文本分解成语步。有些文本清楚地有着首要和次要目的。

风格是指系统的美学偏好。我们都有某些口语和书面语语言偏好，有些语料库分析专家关注的是那些可以被用来界定一个特定作者作品的风格偏好。莎士比亚的戏剧被分析，用来界定那些由合著者编写的部分，他们的词汇语法偏好和原著不同。

我们用来界定语域、体裁和风格的标志和某个外延有交叉。比如，academic可能指情境变量，包括科学话题、正式的书面语或某个交际目的，来宣告新知识，甚至可以用来表达个人写作风格。然而，当用在专业角度时，其语域、体裁和风格是不同的，并且对语料库的设计和检索也有不同的意义，如表11.1所示。

表11.1 Comparing Register, Genre & Style (Biber, et al., 2009)

Defining characteristic	Register	Genre	Style
Textual focus	Sample of text excerpts	Whole texts	Sample of text excerpts
Linguistic features	Any lexicogrammatical feature	Specialized expressions, rhetorical organization	Any lexicogrammatical feature
Disiribution of linguistic features	Frequent and pervasive in texts from the variety	Seldom occurring; specific to certain pervasive in texts	Frequent and points in the text from the variety
Interpretation	Features serve important communicative functions	Features serve to organise the genre according to conventions	Features are not functional but preferred for aesthetic reasons

对于语域分析，我们主要看样本文本，任何语言特征，词汇或语法，这些特征遍及整个文本，我们假设这些特征是由交际目的形成的。对于体裁分析，因为更多地关注话语结构，我们需要接触所有的文本，看看那些标志着语步的语言学特点（有时被叫做词汇触发），这些特点趋向于发生在话语中的具体位置。我们可以假设这些特征帮助我们实现话语的交际目的。对于风格分析，如语域一样，我们可以用文本样本来分析，任何词汇语法特点都可以被看作美学偏好，这些特点遍及全部文本，它们可以作为偏好的证明（而不是情境或目的）。

在线练习

用COCA中的图表功能（图11.1）来探究语域分析。检索结果如图11.2所示，是get passive的比率（像he got caught而不是he was caught）。

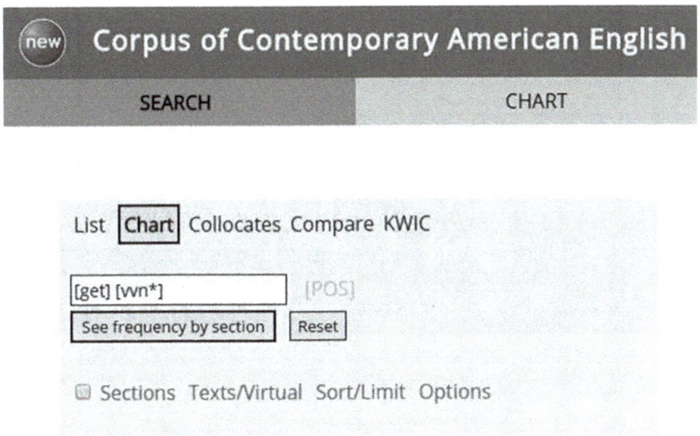

图 11.1

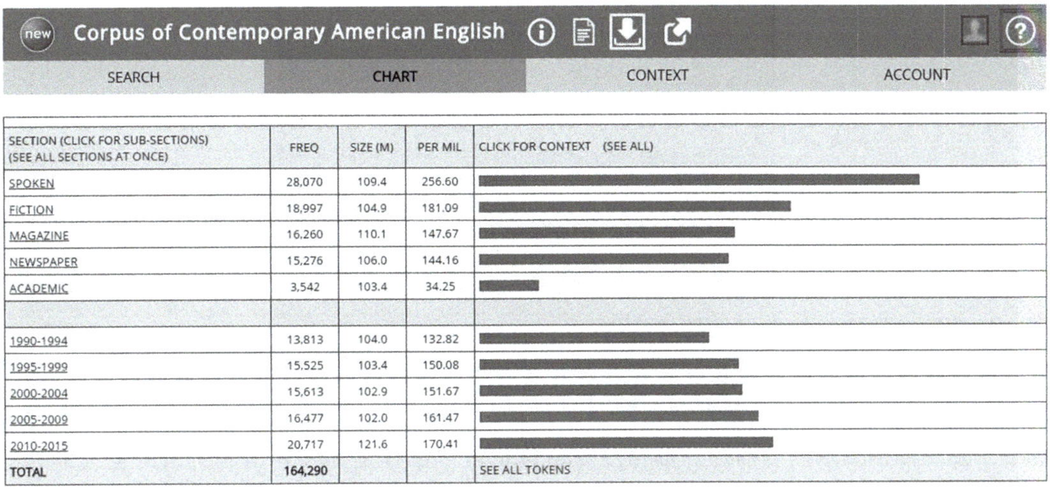

SECTION (CLICK FOR SUB-SECTIONS) (SEE ALL SECTIONS AT ONCE)	FREQ	SIZE (M)	PER MIL	CLICK FOR CONTEXT (SEE ALL)
SPOKEN	28,070	109.4	256.60	
FICTION	18,997	104.9	181.09	
MAGAZINE	16,260	110.1	147.67	
NEWSPAPER	15,276	106.0	144.16	
ACADEMIC	3,542	103.4	34.25	
1990-1994	13,813	104.0	132.82	
1995-1999	15,525	103.4	150.08	
2000-2004	15,613	102.9	151.67	
2005-2009	16,477	102.0	161.47	
2010-2015	20,717	121.6	170.41	
TOTAL	164,290			SEE ALL TOKENS

图 11.2

如图 11.2 所示，get passive 更多地是口语和小说的特征与学术书面语进行比较。语料库的检索结果证明了我们的判断：这是口语的一个普遍特征并且在正式书面语中避免使用。这种检索用在线语料库很容易实现。

正如前面所说，语料库语言学对地理变量关注得相对较少（这一情况正在转变）。较早关注地理变量的一个语料库是苏格兰文本口语语料库（或者叫苏格兰语料库，图 11.3）。这是个相对较小的语料库，大概 400 万到 500 万词汇，其中 25%是口语。它的内容囊括标准英语到浓重苏格兰英语风格的不同地理变量，所以它可以用来检查和说明很多苏格兰英语的特征。苏格兰语料库的数据不是全面公正或具有代表性的（比如 opportunistically 这个词是 randomly 的夸张说法），所以这就出现了很多关于语料库设计和概括语言变体的可能性的问题，但是这也生动地说明了语言的各个方面和复杂性用在地理基础之上，就像展示语言根据说话人的社会阶级、年龄和性别如何变化。它是人为标记过的，但是你可以检索词汇、短语，检索关键词索引或进行其他形式的在线检索。

苏格兰语料库的书面语部分包括很多对苏格兰议会程序的转写,包括正式报告、正式书面记录(像辩论);有少量的个人文本,例如信件和日记;还有一定数量的已出版或未出版的文字材料。

图 11.3

语料库的口语部分包括讲座、讲话、访谈和非正式对话。像其他文字材料一样,对话从标准英语到浓重的苏格兰风格英语。

使用苏格兰语料库最直接的方法是检索苏格兰口语中有争议的特点(图 11.4),这有可能是词汇,针对特定方言或某种语法特点。这些特点有些在苏格兰方言词典中有记录,还有些在社会语言学文献里有描述。苏格兰方言词汇可以看作是苏格兰语和英语的连续体。

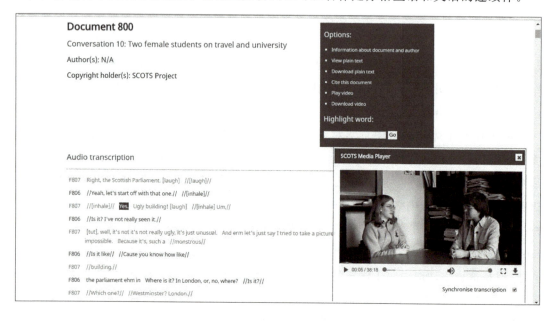

图 11.4

如表 11.2 所示,第 1 列是严格被划为苏格兰方言的词汇,这些词中的有些词可能以前英格兰人也用,但现在完全只被一些苏格兰人使用。第 2 列的词是和第 4 列英格兰英语同源的词,它们有着共同的语源,如"mair/more""stane/stone""hoose/house"等。这些词被苏格兰人和英格兰人共同使用,只是苏格兰方言的形式略有不同。第 3 列的词是苏格兰方言和英语都会使用的,像 winter、some,被两种变体共同使用,苏格兰方言的词汇里没有专门的词来表达这些概念。第 5 列是与第 1 列苏格兰方言对应的英语表达,例如,conspicuous 在苏格兰方言中表达成 kenspeckle。

表 11.2　Aitken's Scots-English continuum

——————Scots——————		Common Core	——————English——————	
1	2	3	4	5
baimn	mair	before	more	child
lass	stane		stone	girl
kirk	hame	name	home	church
chaft	dee	see	die	jaw
gowpen	heid	head	double handful	
ken	hoose	tide	house	know
bide	loose(*n*)	young	louse(*n*)	remain
kenspeckle	louse (*adj*)	winter	loose (*adj*)	conspicuous
low	yaize (*v*)	of	use (*v*)	flame
cowp	yis(*n*)	is	use(*n*)	capsize
shauchle	auld	some	old	shuffle
whae's aucht that?	truith	why	truth	whose is that?
pit the haims on	barra	he	barrow	do in
tummle the wulkies		they		turn somersaults
no (*adv*)	*		not (*adv*)	
-na (*adv*)		+		-n't (*adv*)

* Most of the inflectional system, word order. grammar.
+ Pronunciation system and rules of realisation.

苏格兰语料库告诉我们,语言的用法事实上很复杂。不仅仅是有不同的说英语者,而且这些说英语者在说的时候也是不断变化的。

F643: //Aye, mind they// took it uptae Aberdeen and we gave her ten pound tae buy flowers for the bairn; a wreath and that. And the lassie came back and thanked us hersel,

M608: Aye.

F643: lateron about that.

F643: sh— we used tae take the kids tae her and then I came through here and cleaned aw this place, so I widnae bring the kids, ye see. So, I cleaned aw this place. //Until the kids.//

F643: //She wasfeedin the baby in bed and she// must've slept on it, ye see.

M608: mm

F643: So, and eh, she had three other lovely children.

在上面这段对话中,说话人 F643 来自 Fife(苏格兰地名),我们看到她在其中一个话轮中用了 bairn,在其他话轮中用了 kids 和 children。说话人在苏格兰方言和标准英语中来回转换。

如果我们比较苏格兰语料库中口语部分某些词出现的频率,就会发现第 1 列和第 5 列中的词会同时出现,尽管英语词的原始频率超过跟它对等的苏格兰方言,如表 11.3 所示,比如,Lass 出现了 50 次,而 girl 出现了 424 次。

表 11.3 Number of occurrences of Column 1 and 5 items in SCOTS (spoken)

Column 1		Column 5	
Item	No. of instances in SCOTS(spoken)	Item	No. of instances in SCOTS(spoken)
bairn	133	child	323
lass	50	girl	424
kirk	2	church	83
chaft	0	jaw	5
gowpen	0	double handful	0
ken	717	know	5789

有些偏僻词汇没有计数,即使是在一百万词的语料库中,像 chaf、gowpen 都没有出现。即使是英格兰英语,jaw 也只出现了 5 次。所以,为了得到更好的对苏格兰方言的口语描述图,我们需要更大、更系统的数据体系。

现在从词汇转到语法,我们来看看名词词素,复数是怎么构成的?在很多英语词汇里,通常是在词尾加-s 或-es,但也有一些例外,例如,oxen 或者 children 使用一个古老的英语复数词缀-en。有些苏格兰方言词汇到今天仍使用古英语复数词缀-n,像-een 是-ee (-eye)的复数形式。所以,twa een 在苏格兰方言中意为两只眼睛。在下面这段对话里我们看到一个妈妈在教孩子复数形式。这个妈妈在教五官的名字;鼻子 nose,孩子把复数词缀-een 读成了-eeks。

> F1091: //Now,// //you goin to tell me what is this. //
>
> M1092: //[child noises]// //Nose. //
>
> F1091: //What's that? Aye. // And fitt's this? It's yer e-? //Come here. //
>
> M1092: //Eeks. // Eeks.
>
> F1091: It's yer, is it yer een?
>
> M1092: Myeeks. Eeks, eeks.
>
> F1091: It's nae, it's yer een.

另外,苏格兰方言的语法特点是使用特定的限定词,数字跟着单数名词,所以下面对话中来自 Fife 地区的说话人说 twa hunded pound 和 twa hoose。

> M642: He says, 'Right, I'll need twa hundred pound for it. '
>
> ……
>
> M642: //n—naw! Efter aboot// twa year he says, 'I'm fed up o youse comin up here every week. '
>
> ……
>
> M642: Now, I actually built twa hoose.
>
> BUT:
>
> M642: But see they prefabs, John, over there? //Ye put they//
>
> M608: //Aye. //
>
> M642: prefabs on a flat roof in a runo three inches.
>
> M608: uh—huh
>
> M642: And I pit, I says, 'Right, I'll put twa layers o felt on it. '

像词汇那样,形式变化从苏格兰方言到英格兰英语,后面在同样的对话里,相同的说话人在谈论 three inches 和 twa layers o flet,所以,他用了名词的复数形式和数字结合。

通过观察动词,我们可以建立一幅图,即语法是如何在当代苏格兰方言中发生作用的。一个弱势动词或规则变化的动词,通常会添加曲折词缀-ed,例如 walk 变成 walked。一个强势动词或规则变化的动词,会改变它的中元音或尾元音,所以 sell 变成了 sold,know 变成了 knew。但是在苏格兰方言中的一个不规则变化的动词在英语中可能就是规则变化的。在苏格兰方言中添加 it 或 t 到词干中,比如,selt(sold),或 kennt(knew)。

最后,我们来看看苏格兰口语方言的语法特点,这些特点也出现在非标准英语里,即所谓的缩略动词的模式。大部分常出现的英语动词有两种结构,例如 walk/walked/have walked。强势动词有三种结构,例如 know/knew/known(在 I know/I knew/I have known)中。在苏格兰方言中,和其他变体一样,动词从三种结构变为两种结构,例如,It's went 变为 It's went hard。

和词汇语法特点一样,苏格兰语料库说明了很多独特的话语标记。像 see 用来标记新话题的转换或者话题中的转换。这点可以从下面来自 Fife 的语料贡献者(M642)的口语中得到证实:see yoor hoose 表明话题是关于听话人的家。听话人(M608)回答用的是苏格兰方言的最小标记 aye(是)。

"See" as a topic-marker;"aye" as a response token:

> M642://See your//hoose, John. We'll go on tae that. See your hoose? //Your hoose was eh//
>
> M608://Aye. //
>
> F643:The forester's house.

课后拓展

用 BNC 中的图表功能来探究 get passive(如 get dressed、get caught)的语域分布,并描述检索结果。

典例示范

可以看到,get passive 在口语和小说文本中出现次数较多(图 11.4)。和预想的一样,get passive 比较多地出现在口语文本而非正式的书面语文本中。

SECTION	ALL	SPOKEN	FICTION	MAGAZINE	NEWSPAPER	NON-ACAD	ACADEMIC	MISC
FREQ	9036	3044	2201	805	754	777	354	1101
WORDS (M)	100	10.0	15.9	7.3	10.5	16.5	15.3	20.8
PER MIL	90.36	305.51	138.35	110.85	72.04	47.10	23.09	52.84

图 11.4

a. Yes (pause) we were (pause) there last year because my granddaughter **got married.**

b. the library Oh is it? I thought it was Mhm **Getting mixed up**

c. Do you remember when you **got rid of** one of your armchairs last year or the year before, they bought

d. Can you tell me about the light fittings that you bought when you first **got married**

e. when the War was ending you know. And er she'd tried to **get rid of** it and she couldn't, so she found out her husband was

f. Ah that's a nerve, that's a nerve **getting inflamed up** the back there. Well it took the pain away like that

g. we'll just check that out again, and make sure that that's all **got healed** over.

h. I **got dressed** up in the minister's cassock, and I got in (unclear) revised the

第十二章　语料库和语言教学

语料工具

- AntConc 软件
- 杨百翰大学语料库（BYU）
- 国际学习者语料库（ICLE）

教学内容

语料库语言学对英语教学的影响深远，它改变了教学大纲设计、语言测试、课本内容、教学材料的挑选，以及课堂活动。语料库也被用于二语习得的基础研究。因此，关于语料库的出版物曾经大量出现。

将语料库数据转换成资源或实践以提升教学效果不是一个自然或简单的过程。教育者需要思考很多问题：在什么情况下学习者要接触原始语料？在什么情况下他们能够从数据中归纳出语法特点？是由教师或语料编写者将语料库作为中介介绍给学习者的还是由学习者自己学会使用语料库的？学习者应该被教会元语言吗？他们应该熟悉搭配、关键词索引行、交互信息等等吗？如何期望学习者积极使用语料库数据？他们应该内化这些数据吗？正如我们所看到的，语料库数据让我们认识到语言是错综复杂的，规则可以被打破，那么学习者如何对特殊的、固定不变的规则做出反应？

我们从教师容易忽视的一点入手——一个文本档案馆。有些语料库允许用户获得完整的文本或者大量的文本样本。如果语料库设计得很好，那么我们可以发现原始语言的例子，至少是那些没有被改编成用于教材的语言，或者是教材编写者很难找到出处的语言。一旦选择了输入语言，我们就可以设计一个活动。在 Divid Nunan 所著的 *Designing Tasks for the Communicative Classroom* 一书中，他提到任务具有某种学习目标，用一种输入、一个活动来达到这个目标。学习者在课堂活动中扮演一定的角色，教师也是。学习设置有个人任务，结对练习，小组活动或全班活动。

例如，苏格兰语料库就是对话式讲故事活动的来源。一堂基于语料库的课可以设计成这样：

A. 目的：练习对话式讲故事；

B. 输入：苏格兰语料库中的录音；

C. 活动：预测故事，听对话，注意有用的表达，对自己创作的故事做出相应修改；

D. 学习者的角色:参与,修改;

E. 教师角色:构建任务,监控,指出有用的语言;

F. 设置:结对练习。

输入是听力活动。下面是一个孩子跟父亲的对话,孩子在给父亲讲解卡通人物蝙蝠侠是怎么变成真人的。在听这段对话之前,教师可以让学生进行故事内容预测,并进行角色扮演。

> FATHER:[laugh] Okay. So, ehm, I was wondering if maybe you could tell me about how Spiderman became Spiderman?
>
> CHILD:Ehm, so this guy wa-, called Peter Parker was in a place and officer um [?]crogrammes[/?] and there was a spider,//radioactive//
>
> FATHER://mm//
>
> CHILD:spider.
>
> FATHER:Oh!

这是故事的第一部分。父亲使用很多隐晦的语言 如 I was wondering if maybe,来引导孩子讲出故事。当孩子开始讲故事,父亲用一些反应标记,如 mm、oh 等表示惊讶的词,来鼓励他继续讲述。

在孩子讲故事的时候,他开始偏离一般情节:Peter Parker 变成了蜘蛛侠。父亲核实了这点(通过重复孩子的讲述)。孩子接着讲:Peter Parker 有着蜘蛛的身体和人的脑袋。

> CHILD:And it climbed up Peter Parker and it bit him and then hetu- and then he was poisoned by that spider and he, and he was turning into a spider himself!
>
> FATHER:Oh //He turned in-//
>
> CHILD://[?]Witha[/?]// human head!

同样,父亲核实了孩子讲述(通过疑问语气的重述)。孩子确认了这个故事,父亲进一步推进。孩子很聪明地返回去说这是个梦想,并转到一个新的情节:Peter Parker 走进一条小巷,钻进了一辆开来的汽车。父亲又表示出惊讶。

> FATHER:Oh so he had a spider's body and a human head?
>
> CHILD:Yeah.
>
> FATHER:Oh! So how did he become Spiderman that's not got the spider's body?
>
> CHILD:Um, and there wasactually a dream and a- and he walked onto the road and a car was coming //for him//
>
> FATHER://Oh! //

通过强调 Peter Parker 超人的能力,如能粘在墙上,孩子总结了这个故事,所以他叫自己 Spiderman。

> CHILD: and he jumped and he was sticking to the wall!
> FATHER: Really?
> CHILD: Erm, and he noticed he had superpowers, so he would call himself Spiderman!

学生听完录音后,老师可以让他们比较自己的版本和孩子的版本,不仅仅是内容,还有讲故事的方式。有一点要注意的是,孩子在某些方面比成年人模糊,如 Peter Parker was in a place。父亲用了很多反应标记语和问题来引导孩子讲述。孩子用语调来表达故事的高潮,并使用了元音拖音 Spidermaaaam。

在这些特点被指出并讨论后,学生可以再做一遍这个任务,想象一个小孩在讲述另一个像 Spiderman 的超级英雄。

有些教师发现,在让成年学生扮演小孩的时候,这些学生会感到尴尬、别扭。教师要判断学生对于任务要求做出的反应。

有些语料库可以作为很好的文本档案,但不能用于教科书。像对话故事、商业报道,这些文本有着可预测的结构,积极地使用它们,注意其特点,会有助于内化体裁特征。

Gilquin 和 Paquot(2011)概述了学习英语方面的研究,包括非本族语者在学术写作中"过度使用"和"未充分使用"的争议。一些特点,如人称代词缩写、量词 all 或指示代词 that,和书面语相比,在口语中频繁出现,并且德国人、西班牙人和保加利亚人用得很多。同样,Granger 和 Rayson(2013)证明了说法语者过度使用很多口语中的词汇语法特点,如第一、第二人称代词或短副词(also、only、so、very 等),但是未充分使用正式书面语中的特点,如高密度的名词和介词。其他研究则关注更具体的词目,如 I think、of course、because、so,结果表明这些词目趋向于被学习者过度使用,并且这种过度使用给学习者的写作带来明显的口语特点。

Gilquin 和 Paquot 提供了一个国际学习者语料库词汇过度使用的表格(表 12.1)。无论是本族语者还是非本族语者,如何在写作中使用这些表达都是值得注意的。

表 12.1 Spoken-like overused lexical items per rhetorical function

RHETORICAL FUNCTION	SPOKEN-LIKE OVERUSED LEXICAL ITEM
Exemplification	like
Cause and effect	thanks to so because that/this is why

续表

RHETORICAL FUNCTION	SPOKEN-LIKE OVERUSED LEXICAL ITEM
Comparison and contrast	look likelike
Concession	sentence-final adverb though
Adding information	sentence-initial and adverb besides
Expressing personal opinion	I think to my mind from my point of view it seems to me
Expressing possibility and certainty	really of cour'se absolutely maybe
Introducing topics and ideas	I would like to/want/am going to talk about thing by the way
Listing items	first of all

在已出版的学术文章、学生的论文、学习者的书面语和口语中,学习者和本族语学生都是更趋向于使用 maybe,如图 12.1 所示。换句话说,他们的用法和学术写作相比更接近口语。

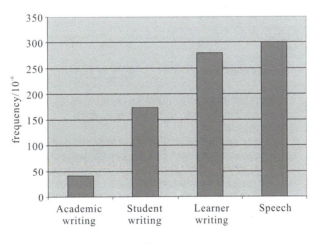

图 12.1

我们可以尝试测试这个表中的数据(在 BNC 或 COCA 这样标准语料库中的出现频率),看看 maybe 在口语和学术语域中出现的频率。

将国际学习者语料库的数据和鲁汶本族语英语写作语料库(图 12.2)对比(鲁汶英语写

作语料库包含 300 000 个英美学生学术论文中的词汇），研究发现初学写作的学生普通趋向于使用口语词汇，不论英语是否是他们的母语。

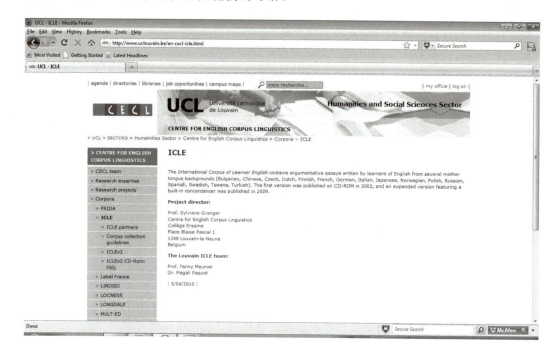

图 12.2

这种基于语料库的研究对于英语学习资源（如学习者词典）来说有影响。查阅 MACMILLAN 在线词典，它建议在正式写作中使用 perhaps，而 maybe 被界定为在口语中和非正式写作中使用（图 12.3）。

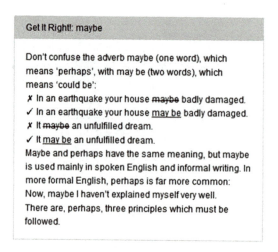

图 12.3

所以，这是学习者语料库中的一种作用：分析一组学习者口语或书面语的使用，并和本族语者的语料库进行对比。然后,我们可以将发现用于课程设计、教材和参考资料中。一个即时的学习者语料库的用途就是给学习者带来益处。教师收集分析一组学习者的数据,然后将数据应用在这组的教学资料中。这个工作强度不大,也不太复杂,很像行为分析,但很有用。

Corbett 教授曾收集了他的 20 个硕士生的课程论文并用在他的语料库中。他们写的是基于语料库的英语习语研究。这些论文被转换为纯文本文件并上传到 AntConc。这是一个小语料库,但很集中。在其中搜索一些被 Gilqin 和 Paquot 界定为过度使用的关键词,可以发现,在这些论文中,有很多像 I think 这样的例子(图 12.4)。

下一步回到 File View 并在更大的语境中搜索 I think(图 12.5)。我们看到 I think 和 because 联用:"And I think this is because…",有意思的是 I think 被用来弱化或隐藏因果关系。在学术英语中这是怎么实现的呢?

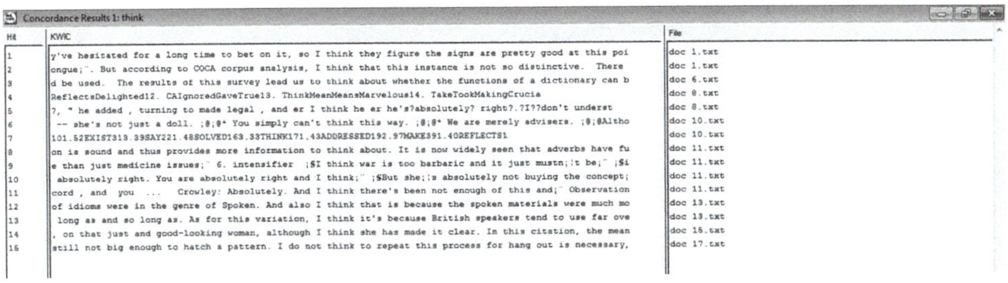

图 12.4

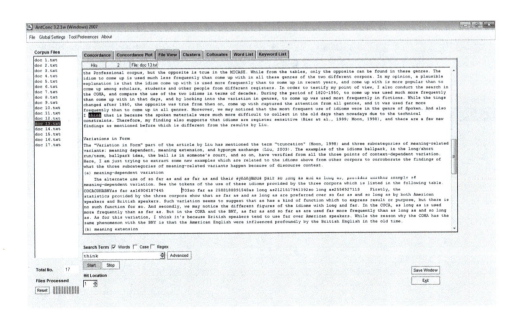

图 12.5

在线练习

在进一步探究中，我们在 BNC 中检索 because 在 ACADEMIC 中的搭配(图 12.6)。because是经常被用来修饰从句结果的弱化词或隐晦词，是副词，所以我们把检索限定为副词。

检索结果如图 12.7 所示，可以看到哪些副词常用在 because 附近。这些短语的表达常在学术写作中用来表达立场和观点。其中，出现频率最高的副词有 partly 和 simply。

图 12.6

		CONTEXT	FREQ
1		PARTLY	332
2		SIMPLY	201
3		ONLY	171
4		PRECISELY	128
5		PERHAPS	125
6		ALSO	116
7		JUST	107
8		LARGELY	97
9		LEAST	92
10		EITHER	82
11		PROBABLY	76
12		MAINLY	65
13		SO	65
14		MERELY	63
15		PART	45
16		POSSIBLY	41
17		HERE	38
18		PRESUMABLY	32

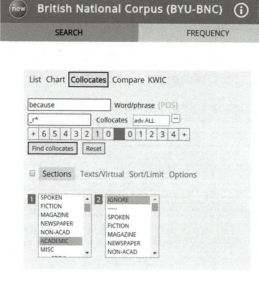

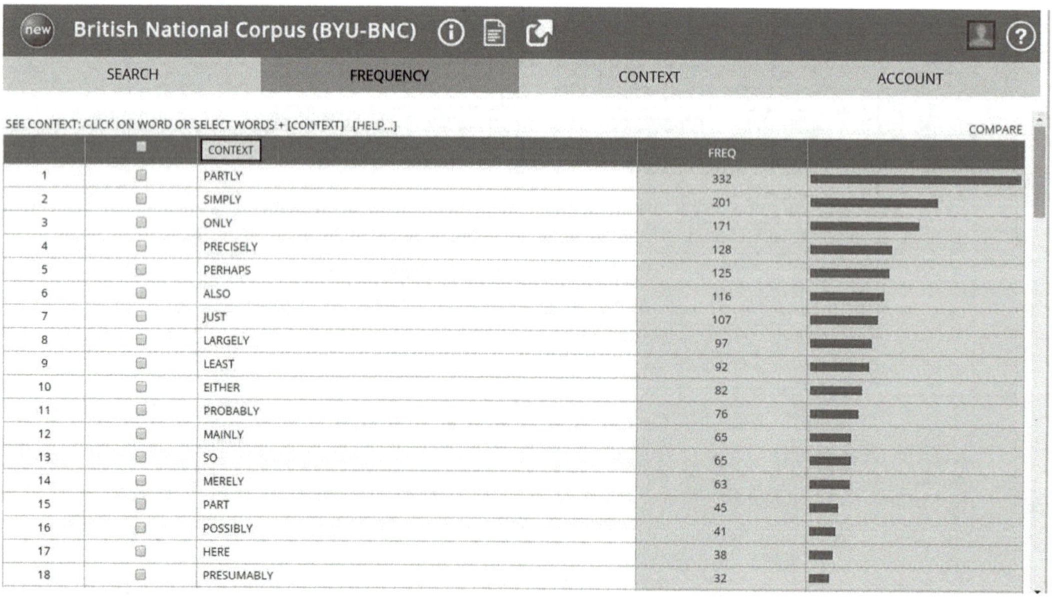

图 12.7

现在的问题是：这些副词中的哪些词在经常在学生写作中被用在 I think 的位置？
例句：

> Moreover we may noticed that the most frequent use of idioms were in the genre of Spoken. And also I think that is because the spoken materials were much more difficult to collect in the old days due to the technical constraints.

当我们看语境时，我们会发现有几个口语标记语在第二句——and 和——also，就像 I think 一样。所以我们可以使用语料库来对论文的这部分进行改写：删除 and also 并用 presumably 代替 I think。例句就变成了：

> Moreover we may noticed that the most frequent use of idioms were in the genre of Spoken, presumably because the spoken materials were much more difficult to collect in the old days due to the technical constraints.

这个过程十分耗费精力，但是随着时间的推移，如果教师把这些改变都记录下来，他就可以建一个学习清单，让学生注意到学术写作中恰当的表达方式。这些资料对于学生很有用。

课后拓展

在 BNC 中检索 because 在 ACADEMIC 中的搭配。

典例示范

如图 12.8 所示，从检索结果来看，经常出现在 because 附近的副词有 partly、only、so、more、also、simply、perhaps、just 等。对于学生来说，写论文的时候就可以参照以上检索结果对自己的论文进行润色，如果使用了不合适的副词，也可以进行修改，让其更符合英语写作的习惯。对于教师来说，汇总整理一些在学术论文写作中经常用到的连词、副词，建立起一个供学习者学习的常见词汇搭配清单，这样在授课和批改论文时也能有比较可靠的参考，对学生学习亦有很大的帮助。

如图 12.9 和图 12.10 所示，经过检索，because 在 NEWSPAPER 中的副词搭配中，出现频率最高的是 so、just、only、up、out、too、very、also、more、now 等。

对于语域分析来说，BNC 的 Collocates 可以让语料库使用者清楚地了解到某一个词在哪些语域中出现得最频繁。

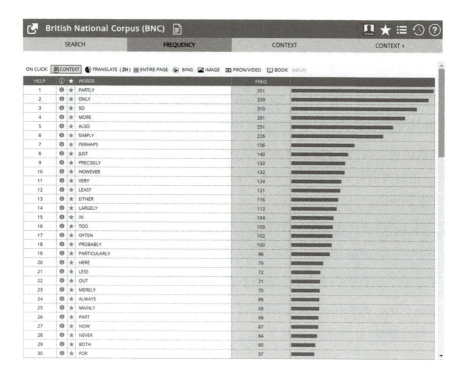

图 12.8

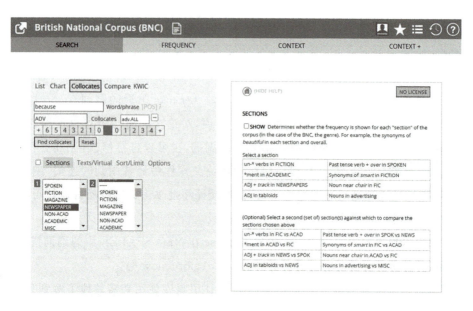

图 12.9

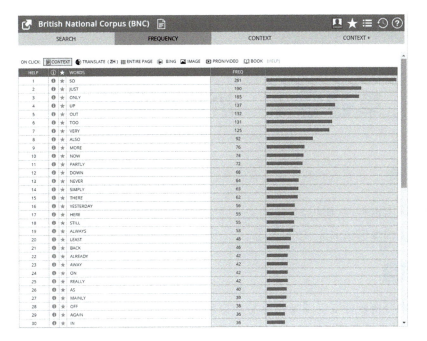

图 12.10

第十三章 语料库设计

语料工具

● 英国国家语料库(BNC)
● 当代美国英语语料库(COCA)

教学内容

由于文本分析软件变得越来越容易获得和使用,因此我们也可以设想建立自己的语料库。本章所讲的内容主要是关于设计语料库的基本理论和代表性实践问题。在开始之前,先来想想这个问题:我们自己的语料库为何而建?

对这个问题有不同的答案,例如:

(1)提供精确口语或书面语语法、词汇、话语和音系学的描述;
(2)帮助非本族语者学习英语;
(3)研究儿童二语习得;
(4)研究特定的体裁、语域;
(5)研究特定地理或社会方言特点;
(6)改进机器翻译;
(7)提高自然语言处理;
(8)研究文化、语言方面的使用(例如关于热点话题,不同的人是如何使用语言表达立场的)。

建立语料库的目的将在很大程度上决定了语料库的类型,以及它的范围、大小、安排、时间等。

语料库设计的先驱 Douglas Biber 在 20 世纪末提出一个实用的语料库设计循环并且进行了改进,从一个先导性实证性研究调查和语言问题的理论分析开始。理想化的方案是,先提出一个研究问题,然后想想需回答这个问题所采用的分析数据的方法;接下来依据需要加以注释,恰当地对它进行标记。

换言之:

(1)确定语言的种类,建构研究问题和分析方法;
(2)设计语料库(使用抽样框架);

(3)用框架编辑语料库;

(4)检查语料库,如有需要即加以改进;

(5)不断重复以上步骤,直到用完建设资金。

当然,这是一个理想化的循环。

更多的情况是,你在一个大的合作团队中,你可能在没有特别具体的研究问题的情况下就开始编辑语料库。比如说这样的问题:我想知道商务会议是什么结构?我想知道电视剧的脚本是什么样的?就像苏格兰语料库,最初的团队只是想看看苏格兰方言的起源。在这种情况下,编辑语料库时可能会撇开像注释和标记开放这些方面。① 使用上面的方法有优势,但也有局限性。

COCA 是一个强大的语料库,可供多种使用者在线使用。它以 BNC 语料库为模型,但是在设计和内容方面与之不同,其中的文本自动使用 CLAWS 做语法分析。兰卡斯特大学的语料库项目也参照了 BNC。语料库的设计理念影响着研究类型,例如语法解码决定了检索的种类。

下面来看看 COCA 的具体结构。

COCA 包括超过 52 000 万个文本词汇,分为口语、小说、杂志、报纸和学术期刊。每年语料库在 5 种语域(口语、小说、杂志、报纸和学术期刊)被均衡划分。

其文本来源很多:

(1)口语:超过 150 种电视广播节目的对话文字转录。需要注意的是,COCA 中所有的口语数据都是来源于不用稿子的媒体广播,这点和其他在线语料库(如 BNC 或苏格兰语料库)不同。

(2)小说:短篇小说和戏剧,来自文学杂志、儿童文学,以及从 1990 年到现在的首版书籍的头几章和电影脚本。

(3)大众杂志:覆盖近 100 种不同的杂志,具体领域包括新闻、健康、家庭、园艺、女性、财经、宗教、运动等。

(4)报纸:涵盖美国地区的 10 种报纸,包括 *USA Today*,*New York Times*,*Atlanta Journal Constitution* 等。

(5)学术期刊:包括近 100 种同行评议期刊。这些被挑选的期刊覆盖美国国会图书馆分类法②的全部系统。

COCA 是一个强大的语料库,意在展示当代标准的美国英语。其他的专业语料库大都比较具体,像澳门口语语料库,大概有 30 小时的访谈,使用英语、葡萄牙语和粤语三种语言;学术口语英语密芝根语料库,是一个集合了不同学术体裁的口语文本语料库,包括讲座、研

---

① 标记开放是指创建一个口语和书面语的文件档案。
② 例如,B 代表哲学、心理学、宗教,D 代表世界历史,K 代表教育,T 代表技术,等等。

讨会、咨询会议等。

无论想建立的语料库是什么语料库,总会有人问这样的问题:这个语料库具有代表性吗?而我们也会问自己:这个语料库够不够大?这些问题回答起来并不容易。

先来想想代表性的问题,代表性是语料库语言学中一个复杂的问题。

我们可以用不同的方式来思考这个问题:

(1)体裁的范例要在所有或某些话语领域具有典型性;

(2)一个语料库要在语言学方面代表一个完整的语言。

Biber认为,在一个语言领域里,一个有代表性的范例包括一套能够代表这一领域特点的体裁。苏格兰语料库即符合这一标准,因为它建立了一个范例框架。然而,语料库的设计者很快发现这样的抽样框架很难实行,比如散文、非小说和论文、日记、文章之间有重叠,需要交叉编码。通常情况下这样也是可行的,因为可以用不同的方式交叉编码,检索文本。比较麻烦的问题是如何界定每一个内容属于什么体裁。我们可以追求平均地分配,比如找到足够多的私人信件来平衡小说,但这并不容易:如何精确地计算这种平衡?当然,抽样范围也会随着时间变化。例如在设计苏格兰语料库的时候,电子邮件只是很小的一种通信类型(那时短信还没有发明)。

决定语言学代表性的步骤有以下几点:

(1)从一系列语域里选择文本样本(例如对话、小说、学术文章等);

(2)选择一系列感兴趣且能够统计的语言标记语(例如名词、人称代词、介词,现在时和过去时标记);

(3)在抽样中统计每一个特点的数量(原始频率);

(4)统计标准化频率(例如每一千个词出现的平均数);

(5)使用统计公式计算标准差;

(6)和其他文本进行对比,看看样本是否典型或具有代表性。

Biber使用用一套不同语域的文本在一个平衡语料库中研究其代表性,并提出了一套规范以代表对话、通俗小说和学术文章。如表13.1所示,在1000个对话(Conversation)词中平均有137.4个名词,标准差是15.6。

表13.1 Biber's figures

Feature	Conversation		General Fiction		Academic prose	
	Mean	SD	Mean	SD	Mean	SD
Nouns	137.4	15.6	160.7	25.7	188.1	24.0
Prepositions	85.0	12.4	92.8	15.8	139.5	16.7
Present tense	128.4	22.2	53.4	18.8	63.7	23.1
Past tense	37.4	17.3	85.6	15.7	21.9	21.1

续表

Feature	Conversation		General Fiction		Academic prose	
	Mean	SD	Mean	SD	Mean	SD
Passives	4.2	2.1	5.7	3.2	17.0	7.4
Wh- relatives	1.4	0.9	1.9	1.1	4.6	1.9
Conditionals	3.9	2.1	2.6	1.9	2.1	2.1

任何一个口语语料库要想具有代表性,需要在1000个词中有121.8～153个名词。其他数字,无论高低,都不具有代表性。要注意的是,小说名词稍多,标准差较大;而学术文章名词很多,与小说比起来标准差较小。我们可以尝试用一系列词汇来计算。

所以,要建一个语料库,需要检测它是否具有代表性,就可以参考Biber的方法。它的数据可以被用来评价其他语料库。表13.2显示了针对BNC采用Biber方法的三种语域的名词频率。

表13.2 Biber's figures and the BNC

Nouns	Conversation		General Fiction		Academic prose	
	Mean	SD	Mean	SD	Mean	SD
Biber	137.4	15.6	160.7	25.7	188.1	24.0
BNC	136.5	—	168.7	—	248.6	—

BNC中的名词平均数和Biber的针对口语、对话和通俗小说语域的先导性试验数据相符,其平均数值刚好在标准差范围内。然而,Biber得出的对于学术文章的数据和BNC的平均数相差很大,标准差在2～3。这不禁让人怀疑,Biber的先导性试验或者BNC的范例是否具有代表性。

从以上讨论中可以学到什么?第一,代表性意味着很多东西。语料库创建者应该意识到有很多方式可以处理代表性的问题。对于偏好统计的人,可以用数据界定一个抽样是否具有特定的语言学代表性。第二,不同的抽样大小有不同的特点。例如,很小的抽样需要对普通语法特点具有代表性;而更大的样本则要对更普遍的词汇具有代表性,并且一个很大的语料库有必要对不太普遍的词汇也具有代表性。

当我们决定建一个自己的语料库,并且正在为它的代表性所烦恼时,不必过早纠结统计的问题。我们可以从研究问题开始,建一个文本框架和需要处理的范例的语域,后面再决定统计数据的代表性。

参考文献

ANDERSON W, CORBETT J, 2017. Exploring English with Online Corpora[M]. Palgrave: Macmillan.

BIBER D, CONRAD S, 2009. Register, Genre, and Style[M]. Cambridge: Cambridge University Press.

CHAMBERS A, 2007. Popularising Corpus Consultation by Language Learners and Teachers[M]// HIDALGO E, QUEREDA L, SANTANA J. Corpora in the Foreign Language Classroom. Amsterdam: Rodopi: 3-16.

COURTNEY R, 1993. Longman Dictionary of Phrasal Verbs[M]. Boston: Addison-Wesley.

GARDNER D, DAVIES M, 2007. Pointing out Frequent Phrasal Verbs: A Corpus Based Analysis[J]. TESOL Quarterly, 41(2): 339-359.

GILQUIN G, PAQUOT M, 2011. A Taste for Corpora[M]. Amsterdam: John Benjamins.

GRANGER S, RAYSON P, 2013. Automatic Lexical Profiling of Learner Texts[M]// GRANGER S. Learner English on Computer. New York: Routledge: 119-131.

O'KEEFFE A, MCCARTHY M J, CARTER R A, 2007. From Corpus to Classroom: Language Use and Language Teaching[M]. Cambridge: Cambridge University Press.

SINCLAIR J, 1991. Corpus, Concordance, Collocation[M]. Oxford: Oxford University Press.